YOU ARE THE ONE AND ONLY

Unleash Your New Niche

Discover the power of combining your diverse skills
and experiences to achieve extraordinary success

Mohamed Ali Shukri

World Championship of Public Speaking Finalist
Certified Transformational Leader

Chennai • Bangalore

CLEVER FOX PUBLISHING
Chennai, India

Published by CLEVER FOX PUBLISHING 2025
Copyright © Mohamed Ali Shukri 2025

All Rights Reserved.
Paperback ISBN: 978-93-67078-47-1
Hardcover ISBN: 978-93-67071-30-4

This book has been published with all reasonable efforts taken to make the material error-free after the consent of the author. No part of this book shall be used, reproduced in any manner whatsoever without written permission from the author, except in the case of brief quotations embodied in critical articles and reviews.

The Author of this book is solely responsible and liable for its content including but not limited to the views, representations, descriptions, statements, information, opinions and references ["Content"]. The Content of this book shall not constitute or be construed or deemed to reflect the opinion or expression of the Publisher or Editor. Neither the Publisher nor Editor endorse or approve the Content of this book or guarantee the reliability, accuracy or completeness of the Content published herein and do not make any representations or warranties of any kind, express or implied, including but not limited to the implied warranties of merchantability, fitness for a particular purpose. The Publisher and Editor shall not be liable whatsoever for any errors, omissions, whether such errors or omissions result from negligence, accident, or any other cause or claims for loss or damages of any kind, including without limitation, indirect or consequential loss or damage arising out of use, inability to use, or about the reliability, accuracy or sufficiency of the information contained in this book.

Appropriate permission must be taken from Mohamed Ali Shukri before any reproduction or translation or reference to this book or its contents.

All rights reserved. No part of this book may be reproduced or used in any manner without the written permission of the copyright owner except for the use of quotations in a book review.

Cover page design by Syed Touqeer Ali with inputs from Mohamed Ali Shukri.

DEDICATION

To the 'One and Only' Ali, my late father,
who miraculously made me realize
that I am the 'One and Only'.
And you are the 'One and Only'!

ACKNOWLEDGEMENTS

*T*his book wouldn't have been possible without the dedication and support of these wonderful people who have surrounded and supported me. To each one of them, I want to express my sincerest thanks and gratitude.

My wife and children: For their unwavering love and support, and for being the integral parts of who I am and the difference I strive to make.

Salman Al Rahma: My lifelong friend and mentor, who has helped me stay true to 'The One And Only' value and principle since its inception in 2013—true as a human who lives it, as a speaker who inspires audiences, and as an author who wrote this book.

Manju K. Manohar: For holding my hand every step of the journey to turn this book from a dream into a reality. Her coaching was instrumental in achieving my goal in a structured, organized, and timely manner, with specific guidance on marketing and publishing.

Raymond Pereira: For always pushing me to push my limits, including getting this book to the light. Also, for helping with the illustrations in this book.

Dagmara Pluta: For her ongoing support in the writing process. Long before she contributed to the editing process, her belief in me as a writer helped me overcome my doubts and move forward with actually writing it.

Claire Cosgrove: For her valuable support and contribution towards the editing process.

Sarah Ibrahim: For her steadfast support and contribution towards the editing of the book.

Syed Touqeer Ali: For his magical touch in designing the book cover.

Tissa Dissanayaka: For being there for me, shoulder to shoulder, in shaping and sharpening critical phases of 'The One And Only' program and book.

The Cleverfox Publishing Team: For their support during the publishing process.

And last but not least, to everyone who was and is a direct or indirect reason this book has come to light.

Yours sincerely,

Mohamed Ali Shukri

TABLE OF CONTENTS

Acknowledgements 5
About the Author..9
What Others Say About Mohamed Ali Shukri 11
Introduction 13

Part 1: Manama: Where The Magic Began...17

1. The Firsts..19
2. Gain it All 27
3. Time to Leave 41
4. Lose it All...51

Part 2: Saudi Arabia: A Big Yes To Living Big..59

5. The Project...61
6. Why Me? 67
7. Trash To Treasure.......................................77

Part 3: Mumbai & Mangalore: Miracles 85

8. From Manama to Mumbai 87

9. Miracles in Mangalore 101

10. The 'OAO' Factor 121

11. You Are The One And Only 159

A Note to the Readers 177
Appendix 179

ABOUT THE AUTHOR

MOHAMED ALI SHUKRI

Mohamed Ali Shukri (MBA, CTL, AS, DTM) is the first person from the Middle East to reach the Toastmasters International 'World Championship of Public Speaking' finals. He achieved this feat in Washington DC (2006). In 2020, he also became the first from the Middle East, and the 88th globally, to have earned the coveted 'Accredited Speaker' designation from Toastmasters International. Between and beyond his 'first' and 'best' accolades,

Mohamed learned how to be the 'only', 'The One And Only'.

By opening up to what life has to offer, and what he can offer life, Mohamed found a lot of joy in allowing the flow of his gifts and talents to expand and take creative shapes and forms in the valleys of the world he saw and served.

This resulted in an extraordinarily successful career made by what seemed to be ordinary dots initially. Mohamed's diverse skills and experiences came together in inventive ways, and ended up taking him to play key roles, in key projects, with key clients across the world. 'Play' therefore became the secret and center of Mohamed's career philosophy.

His message to the readers is: "By staying true to yourself, being appreciative of all that you have, and putting it in the service of the betterment of the world and humans, you will live a profound, profitable, and peaceful life."

WHAT OTHERS SAY ABOUT MOHAMED ALI SHUKRI

Mohamed Qahtani
World Champion of Public Speaking (2015)

I have been privileged to attend Mr. Shukri's workshop and be trained by him. In fact, his training is a big reason why I was able to win the world championship. And to have his wisdom in a book format is an opportunity that should not be missed.

Cyril Junior X
World Champion of Public Speaking (2022)

Mohamed had the audience eating from his palm with an enthralling keynote: 'The One And Only'. Even today, I catch myself quoting lines from the keynote in my everyday life. A once in a lifetime experience!

Ron C. McKinnon

Safety consultant, trainer and author

Mohamed is one of the best public speakers and motivators I have had the pleasure of meeting. He shares his personal experience with the audience which they can relate to. His book will be as entertaining as he is.

Paddy Kennedy

Founder/CEO Kennedy Communication Studio International

Working alongside Mohamed Shukri has been one of the most inspiring professional experiences of my career. His ability to connect with individuals, inspire teams, and shape leaders in profound ways has always set him apart. Now, with 'You Are The One And Only', Mohamed brings the essence of his philosophy to life—a philosophy I've seen him live and embody through his extraordinary speaking and training skills.

INTRODUCTION

Are you still searching for your true north?

Are you still trying to discover your true worth?

Owning many talents and experiences, but not knowing where they fit best in the vast job market and business world?

You're not alone.

Work and Worry

Work will consume most of our lives. We worry when we don't have work. When we do have work, we experience a different kind of worry.

Students entering college begin to worry about what they should major or minor in. College students panic about their future jobs before they even graduate. Workers wonder if they are in the right job or the right workplace. Job seekers, business owners, employees, and employers all face the same conflict: "The talents I have versus the talents the market needs. There are many choices available. I've made many choices in my life. But I have ONE career!"

The real challenge for every professional lies in being trapped within the following triangle:

- Opportunities in the market are rapidly increasing.
- My experience, skills, and strengths continue to grow.
- The time I have left is shrinking.

Time, however, is the key element here. It affects ALL THREE sides. As time passes, the market grows larger, your expertise grows bigger, and the time left grows smaller.

Crossroads

Let me get to the heart of the issue. Like me, and many others, you will eventually find yourself at a 'crossroads[1]' where you see three roads but can only take one:

---

[1] Crossroads: an intersection of two or more roads.

1. Pick one area of expertise and drop all others.
2. Pick ALL your areas of expertise and be everything for everyone.
3. Drop ALL your areas of expertise and start a new profession.

The answer is: None of the above.

What if I told you there's a fourth way? A way where, whenever there's a call for a strength or solution you possess, not only will you be chosen, but you'll be 'The One And Only'.

Why this book?

'You Are The One And Only' will show you that no matter what shape, form, or phase your life is in, it hasn't been a random throw of the dice. It has been a jigsaw puzzle. You have 'ALL' the pieces—no more, no less – to reserve a distinct place in the world of work.

How Will You Benefit?

For the past 10 years, I've delivered 'The One And Only' speaking program to thousands at conferences, events, and courses. It quickly gained attention and became a bestseller.

What stood out the most was a particular group of attendees. While feedback was positive across various sectors, this group not only expressed how deeply they were inspired but also reported life-changing results after adopting the program's ideas.

These individuals, from diverse backgrounds—lawyers, business leaders, engineers, teachers, consultants, and more—shared one goal: to further invest their expertise in the best possible opportunities.

Are You Ready?

As you read this book, I can't tell you exactly when or how 'it' will happen to you, too. By 'it' I mean the wake-up call that the attendees of 'The One And Only' program experienced. But I am certain 'it' will. And your 'it' will be unique to you as 'it' was unique to them.

In every chapter, you will read what others went through and how they transformed. You will have your own 'it'. And when you do, your world will appear to you in plain sight, guiding you to your perfect place.

PART 1

Manama: Where The Magic Began

CHAPTER 1

THE FIRSTS

The Gate

From the office gate, my car was parked only twenty meters away, but it was the longest twenty meters I had ever walked in my life.

What happened to me the man who quit his job with no other offer on the horizon?

In that car park, my 40 years of life went on hold. Dozens of unanswered questions pounded my head:

"What now?"

"Who am I now?"

"Where am I?"

"Where do I go from here?"

"Who will want me or my skills?"

"Where do I belong?"

"Where do I fit in?"

"What is my identity?"

"What is my worth? Do I have any?"

Have you ever been there?

Have you ever had such thoughts?

Have you ever had to go through such an experience?

Why don't I take you to where it all began! The Firsts!

*** *** ***

First Things

When we're young, we rarely pause to think before deciding to take on the next thing.

We often choose the first academic pathway, the first job, and it's not surprising if our first spouse is also our first love.

We believe we made all those choices, yet in hindsight, we often realize they were made for us. Yes, it is we who make the final decision with free and full will, but many factors influence our choice.

> We believe we made all those choices, yet in hindsight, we often realize they were made for us.

At 17, my life was a combination of choices; choices I didn't make and choices I did make. I didn't get to choose my parents, to start with.

My father was an educated hardworking man, and a professional in the field of air fueling. My mother graduated from high school and for a while worked as a nurse in a government hospital. She was a smart and lively woman and a dedicated housewife. With them, I had a happy childhood. They let me play and learn naturally by allowing me to express my talents in any form I liked or invented.

First College

But then it was time for a big choice: college. I had no clue which one to join. What does a clueless teenager do in such a case? You guessed it right — asks a close person: a parent, an uncle or aunt. My father didn't leave me much time to think.

"Mohamed, go for Engineering—Electrical Engineering," he told me. "I promise you will have plenty of job opportunities."

Could dad be wrong? Very unlikely, I thought. After all, everybody follows this path: school, college, job, family, children, house, etc.

So I followed my father's advice and joined the Electrical Engineering College of the University of Bahrain in 1988. Did I like it? Not really. But I convinced myself that this is the path everyone goes through. All I had to do is get through the 4 academic years in order to get the job my father promised I would.

First Job

Spending 4 years of my youth in college was one thing, but studying a subject I didn't like was the worst thing; a complete torture. The best part, however, I did get a job, not long after finishing college. An operator in a power station inside a big factory. Well, I guess dad was right. Did I like my new job? Who cared? I needed to validate the fact that I could get a job after studying. I needed to prove to myself, my parents, and others that I was successful. Any delay in moving to the next step in my career might have meant I was a 'loser' or 'no good' for whatever others expected of me. So, I chose not to be that person. Plus, who would reject an opportunity like this? A decent job at a large company with a decent pay? For many young people in my generation, this was a dream job.

First Lady

In addition, this job made me ready for the next step: marriage. I now can propose to the girl of my dreams. Choosing my life partner was something I took more seriously and carefully than the first college or the first job.

However, this lady – my current wife – was a lady I couldn't afford to let go and not get engaged to. She, in other words, was, and still is, the 'first lady' in all positive senses the phrase carries. I couldn't get any luckier, I thought back then, and I still believe that after 30 years of our marriage.

***

"After attending 'The One And Only' program, I experienced a complete paradigm shift. Tasks I once considered time-wasting and trivial, at home and work, now seem like precious opportunities to develop my skills for a better future. Even mundane activities, such as meetings with customers, writing reports, and doing dishes, are now seen as stepping stones toward a brighter tomorrow."

– Zainab Mohamed
Banker, Bahrain

*** *** ***

Take A Moment And Think:

- What were your <u>firsts</u>: in education, career, relationships, and other main aspects of your life?
- Which firsts lasted, and which ones ended at certain points?
- Which firsts are you grateful for, and which ones do you regret?
- Whether your firsts lasted or ended, have they influenced the life you have now? In what ways?
- If any of your 'firsts' have the potential to positively impact your current life, which ones would they be? Are you open to reviving them in a way that serves your present situation?

Your thoughts here:

*** *** ***

CHAPTER 2

GAIN IT ALL

Finally, Promoted!

Happy wife! Happy life!

What more could I ask for?

I know! I needed to make a good living to support my wife and our life. My job was good enough. But after we had our first and second child, increasing my income became imperative.

However, staying in my position as a non-supervisory employee meant there was little to no significant improvement in my income. The nominal annual increment was just not enough.

I needed a promotion. But promotions in the department were slower than tortoises. There had to be a way out. And yes, finally there was, literally.

With the company's new expansion project, there were numerous opportunities for transferring, repositioning, and cross-departmental promotions. I applied for every internal supervisory-level vacancy, regardless of the job or department. Finally, I was accepted into the Safety Department.

Unleashed Talent

"Safety! How difficult could that be?" I thought.

All of us — employees — observed safety rules and precautions, more or less. What was different now was that I would be working in a department where I would observe *others* following the company rules.

Simple? No, it wasn't!

It took me a couple of months in the new job to discover that whatever we knew about occupational safety was just the tip of the iceberg. In my previous job, I primarily dealt with machines that would do whatever I commanded them to do using the control panel.

On the other hand, as a safety practitioner, I had to deal mostly with people over whom I had no command. Yet, my mission was to 'make them' comply with the measures that kept them and their co-workers safe at all times.

The safety management systems do ensure that the stipulated policies and procedures—along with responsible leadership—would 'enforce' compliance.

However, a deeper and more sustainable compliance demanded more than the carrot-and-stick approach.

Communication — effective, compelling and persuasive communication — is key to taking all those policies and measures from ink to implementation, from principles to practice. Since a safety practitioner's primary tools are the corporate communication channels—such as safety inductions, meetings, presentations, briefs, workshops, and committees—each of us in the safety team had no choice but to raise the quality of our delivery to the maximum if we wanted to achieve the best compliance results.

This was where my hidden talent surfaced. From the reactions of my manager, colleagues, and the audiences attending my safety talks and training, I had to accept the fact that I demonstrated a level of communication that was exceptional, to say the least. Joining the company's Toastmasters[2] Club only reinforced this discovery.

In my attempt to further polish my presentation skills, in August 2004, I joined the company's Toastmasters Club. I was amazed at the fact that there actually was an international body that helps enhance the leadership and communication skills of hundreds of thousands of its members around the globe. Through consistent practice,

---

[2] Toastmasters International is a nonprofit educational organization that teaches public speaking and leadership skills through a worldwide network of clubs. Please refer to the appendix for further details.

I became the club's – and later the country's – rising speaking star in a short time.

More Skills

I can't stress enough how huge the transition was between my previous job – as a plant operator – and my new job – as a safety practitioner. It was like comparing walking in the meadows to climbing the mountains. A typical safety practitioner's day is a 360 degrees involvement in everything and anything that goes under 'managing, leading, and maintaining a safe workplace'. The critical part was that I had to achieve this through *others*; as inherently safety practitioners face the challenge of ensuring the safety and well-being of individuals who are not under their direct supervision. 'Others' was, therefore, the code I needed to crack, if I wanted safety 'codes' to be practiced, consistently and continually.

A whole lot of 'other skills' were needed to deal with 'others'! It wasn't strange, therefore, to observe myself having to grow my people skills.

> A whole lot of 'other skills' were needed to deal with 'others'!

Some of the strengths that I needed to develop in order to impact hundreds of individuals daily were:
- Active and empathetic listening

- Building genuine rapport
- Establishing meaningful relationships
- Assertiveness
- Agility
- Motivation
- Effective Leadership
- Communication

That was on a typical day. But did I mention that we were in an expansion project? The company, and every employee, were going through an abnormal and highly demanding and challenging phase. I wouldn't exaggerate if I said that all the skills, duties and challenges I had mentioned previously were often multiplied by 2, 3, and 5 times (in some extreme pressuring occasions, even 10 times) due to the abnormality of the phase that my company was going through.

More Certificates

Competence is not just experience! The knowledge you gain from various credible sources is crucial. With no background in safety management, I was fortunate to support my daily field experience with certified courses from trusted and recognized international bodies. My department was generous enough to send me to both short and long courses, allowing me to obtain qualifications in organizational safety management and culture, professional occupational health and safety accreditations, safety standards lead auditor programs and more.

> Competence is not just experience.

One particular certification was related to a specific Safety Management System. Let me call it 'SMS'. My company adopted it in order to uplift the quality of compliance and safety culture as a whole. It was a transitional strategy essential for that stage of what my organization adopted as 'continual improvement'. My colleagues and I, the safety practitioners of the company, were required to become 'SMS approved auditors' so that we could teach and implement it company-wide.

It wasn't a popular accreditation though, not on the wider global scale. I personally would have preferred being a safety practitioner who had been accredited by a more credible and recognized international system. A certification coming from 'ISO[3]' or a similar organization would have looked much more elegant on my CV, and more appealing to future recruiters.

You don't always get what you want, do you? Especially if your employer wants you to take this task and not that, do this, and not that.

---

[3] International Organization for Standards.

> You don't always get what you want, do you? Especially if your employer wants you to take this task and not that, do this, and not that.

"This is life," I thought to myself. Nonetheless, at least I was blessed to have another qualification on my CV. Things were good.

The Pinnacle

What about speaking? Remember I mentioned that I had joined a Toastmasters Club in the company? What I didn't say is that Toastmasters International organizes an annual 'World Championship of Public Speaking' tournament. It takes place every year, during the organization's annual convention in the month of August. Between 25-30 thousand members enroll in this contest. They go through 5 qualifying and rigorous stages to book a spot as a 'finalist' in the final round. And then only one contestant goes on to win the trophy and the coveted title: Toastmasters International World Champion of Public Speaking.

Just a year after joining the club, I became eligible to enter the 2005-2006 International Speech Contest (the speaking contest category that leads to the coveted title mentioned earlier). I started competing from the 'Club level', then progressed to the 'Area level', then the

'Division level' (all of Bahrain), then the 'District level' (All of the Middle East countries put together).

Finally, I reached the finals. I had already qualified for the semifinals, which took place on August 23rd 2006 in Washington DC (where the annual convention was held), and I won that level too. I secured my place among the 'Top Ten Finalists'. I was on cloud nine!

On that Saturday morning (26th of August, 2006), I made history as the first Arab and the first Toastmaster member from the Middle East to reach the World Championships finals.

I desired and fought hard for achieving the coveted 'First place winner' tag. Sadly, it did not happen. However, reaching this far and becoming top 10 in the world – in my first attempt – was a historical feat. My family, my company, my country, and the Toastmasters members in the Middle East all celebrated this success.

My company highlighted this accomplishment in its own way, and I appeared in the internal newsletters for at least two months.

The PR department featured me in Bahrain's newspapers and TV news channels. It was evident, from the reactions of the company's employees and management, that this safety guy (me) was the company's pride. My Safety Department, and especially my manager saw this as not separate from the fact that speaking proficiently and persuasively was much needed in our day-to-day interactions as safety practitioners, and he often emphasized that Mohamed Shukri brought this idea home!

What more?

I had no concrete evidence that this development had directly led to my promotion to the next level: Safety Superintendent. I was mindful of my communication, ensuring it complemented rather than conflicted with my other duties.

The increasing requests and invitations by the various department managers to speak to their employees, and to guide, educate, train and motivate them were neither a surprise nor a secret. Studies show that at least 60% of any safety practitioner's success depends on his or her effective communication. This led me to believe that I would soon be promoted to the position of Safety Superintendent in 2008.

What's next?

Life couldn't have been better. There I was, a successful safety professional who had achieved career heights in just 6 years since the shift. A decently paid job, a prime position, a wide range of skills and qualifications, a growing happy family, and a reputation that was skyrocketing, thanks, exceptionally, to the public speaking accolade.

I simply had gained it all.

Can you blame me for aiming for the next feat in my career?

Regardless, there was no reason for me to dismiss even the highest and most desirable accomplishments as my next goal. After all, my performance had proven it; my popularity had worked in my favor; my parents, my wife and my five children expected nothing less than that for me! I even had some external offers for joining other organizations. I could –and actually needed to— boost my career and take it to the next level. All signs were pointing in that direction.

All signs except one, one big signpost that said: STOP.

It was a dead-end.

***

"In 2018, I attended Mohamed Ali Shukri's 'The One And Only' workshop in Colombo, Sri Lanka. It transformed my view on personal development, highlighting the non-linear nature of professional growth. The workshop helped me appreciate all my experiences and realize my unique qualities as strengths. It empowered me to embrace being 'The One and Only'. I highly recommend this program to anyone seeking to understand and harness their distinctive professional identity."

**– Tissa Dissanayaka Founder,
Boston Negotiation Group, Sri Lanka**

*** *** ***

Take A Moment And Think:

- What have been your career highs, in terms of achievements, landmarks, milestones, and peak accomplishments?
- What qualifications, certifications, courses and further training have you completed to boost your expertise at different points in your career?
- Which of your talents and gifts have gained momentum and bigger growth - thanks to working in a particular organization?
- Have there been talents and skills you did not notice or identify before your employment that came to light and or developed due to the duties and responsibilities you engaged in at work? What were they?
- Have there been specific skills and segments of your performance that an organization you worked for identified or acknowledged as your 'strengths'? Can you list the top five of those strengths?

Your thoughts here:

*** *** ***

CHAPTER 3

TIME TO LEAVE

A Big Wall

Downsizing!

It was no longer a rumor. The company was getting ready for a massive downsizing phase. Various schemes were devised to help the company's safe and smooth transition amidst a period of critical global economic turmoil. Restructuring, relocating, releasing, and reducing came in the form of reasonable, and often attractive packages for the impacted employees. The goal was to encourage employees – at all levels – to take the decision and direction that was in their and their company's best interest.

I started seeing vast and rapid changes: names disappearing and new names appearing. I kept following the news daily, hearing updates from colleagues, and showing little interest. I didn't feel the changes concerned me.

"Where will I be?" was the talk doing the rounds among almost everyone around me. Not me, I didn't have a choice to make – or did I?! "No, not at all!" I thought. The company's decision to offer a compelling package was a wise one for those who could afford to leave and let go of their future career plans in the company.

"I can't! Not me! To leave the company – at this early stage of my career – is not an option. Why am I even thinking of this?!" Yet, the idea kept storming into my head. Was it because my career succession plans had hit a wall? Afterall, getting promoted to the next managerial level or expecting a higher pay were no longer viable amidst the company's downsizing. Moreover, I considered myself lucky enough to still have my current job in the same department and not be subjected to any transfer or even termination. To aim beyond that was - at best - a fantasy.

Crossroads

At the age of 39, and after only 16 years of employment, what choices did I really have? Taking the package and leaving wasn't that appealing to me, at least not financially. My years of work hadn't resulted in a compensation large enough to justify the risk of being out of the job market—even temporarily.

"Don't even think about it," my closest colleagues firmly told me, when I loudly contemplated a hypothetical scenario of 'What if I leave?'. "You are too young for this!" they insisted. "This isn't for you. It's for those who have many years under their belts, who can enjoy substantial financial rewards and receive a pension at the same time. Your years of service entitle you to none of these benefits. Plus, you are a rising star in the company, and we can clearly see you becoming a leader at the next level. Just wait for this storm to pass!"

Absolutely and obviously, there was no doubt what they said was rational and right. All the data and facts supported it. Moreover, if I could just wait until this downsizing was over, I might get back on track and pursue the career progression that was on hold at the moment.

Rain of Voices

The voices that boldly told me NOT TO DO IT were overwhelming. My family—my wife and five children, along with my parents and siblings—surrounded me to ensure I didn't take this foolish decision. No one does this without a solid calculation of the risks and losses. I wasn't eligible for a legal pension; my years of service fell three years short of qualifying for the minimum pension scheme and wage.

> The voices that boldly told me NOT TO DO IT were just overwhelming.

Amidst all that, there I was standing tall yet bowing my head down towards my chest, tuning into my heart, trying to hear its quiet whispers:

- "It's time to leave, Mohamed, it's time to leave".
- "Why?" I replied. "Give me a solid reason. All the evidence on the surface says I shouldn't even think about it!"
- "Well then, why are you thinking about it? Why is the idea crossing your mind, haunting you, and refusing to leave?"
- "It visits everyone in the circumstances we go through, I am no different!"
- "True, but it's different for you. I know that, and you know that. You're not thinking what they're thinking. It's really not about how much money will end up in your bank account. You're just pretending to do the calculations, to go with the flow. Whereas you have a calculation of your own — a risk-and-reward system others aren't thinking of, and you know what I mean."
- "But.. but if I listen to this sole voice and do the unimaginable and unreasonable, I would look stupid to everyone, and .. unfair to my loved ones."
- "But you will stay true to yourself. Isn't this a big enough reason?"
- "True to myself?! Does it really matter? It's not the first time I've had to give up my deepest desires in order to fit into the social norms, family path, and what everyone else longed and loved for me."
- "You're almost 40. You have a one-time chance to fly high and away to wider skies and spaces, like you

always wanted. The only difference is: unlike now, no doors were open before."

- "Yes, yes, yes. My wings are flapping all the time, but the walls were too many, and the roofs were too low for me to soar and fly. But fly to where? There is no place outside waiting for me? There is no time to plan a safe next destination?"
- "Well, isn't life an adventure, Mohamed?"
- "Of course, but what if I do it and regret it?!"
- "What if you don't do it and regret it? Which regret would be more devastating and lasting? To regret leaving or to regret staying?"

> What if you don't do it and regret it? Which regret would be more devastating and lasting? To regret leaving or to regret staying?

I couldn't answer that one. Yet, I'd often imagined the scenario, and the thought of regretting my decision to stay always felt more severe and painful.

The Reign of One Voice

All the choices I made, or had made for me, in my life dwarfed next to this one big choice I had to make. Even choosing to do nothing and stay was a choice I would have to live with. It was awkwardly weird that I – the safety professional – had to go through this peculiar thought process to reach a wise decision. For years, my expertise and practice required me to be extra cautious when it came to identifying hazards and calculating risks. It was I who pushed every individual and group in my organization to 'play it safe', to go far in making sure no one got hurt, to expend all efforts so that no one suffered any harm or loss.

And yet, here I was, torn between two ends: one, to stay, which was one hundred percent safe and secure, and no one would get hurt or unhappy; the other, to leave, which was totally uncertain, dangerous, and potentially unsafe. Which safety practitioner would choose the second option? That's not how we do things.

Yet, I had to decide, and decide fast. Ultimately, I needed to silence either my inner voice or the other voices: my inner voice asking me to leave versus all the other voices prohibiting me from leaving – if I wanted to live peacefully with myself again.

Wait! Did I say 'peace'? That word! Strangely, I didn't feel it or find in it the safe option of keeping my job! Ironically, I found myself at complete peace by opting for the other side – the dark and unknown path – where anything could go wrong. Any risk matrix would rank this option as extremely 'High Risk'. Yet, in that unsafe and hazardous side, I saw joy, bliss, and peace!

> Yet, in that unsafe and hazardous side, I saw joy, bliss, and peace.

On the morning of January 17th, 2010, I walked out of my department, to the company's main gate, and handed over my employee badge to the security officer. My car was parked only 20 meters away. They were the longest 20 meters I had ever walked.

But, I never looked back.

***

"I can confidently say this program helps you achieve what once seemed impossible. By following 'The One And Only', I've learned to set ambitious goals and truly aim high in my life."

– Suhail Shaikh
Director, Bahrain

*** *** ***

Take A Moment And Think:

- Have you encountered unexpected, substantial changes in your organization?
- How did you perceive these changes? Did you engage in and respond to them? Was your reaction positive and optimistic or negative and skeptical?
- Did you consider that these changes might accelerate your career toward your bigger goals, or did you remain guarded, fearing they could hinder your own progress?
- Do you carefully weigh the costs and benefits of each career step to ensure 'nothing goes wrong' or do you let your heart join your mind, embrace some risk, and welcome a bit of adventure?
- Which describes you better: "I shape my career around income and quality of LIVING, even if it's not fulfilling," or "I pursue a career that makes me feel ALIVE, trusting that fulfillment and income will follow in unique ways"?

Your thoughts here:

*** *** ***

CHAPTER 4

LOSE IT ALL

Waking Up At 40

What just happened?! Did I actually do this?! No, no, no. This can't be real! That's not what I had dreamed for myself twenty years ago. I could imagine unexpected twists and turns in my career, mostly due to external factors. But a turn as sharp as this one, totally by my own will and desire?! That wasn't even in my wildest nightmares.

So, I did it. Now what? What's the next move? Where to? Who will be interested in me or my talents and expertise? How am I going to feed my family? I had taken the decision to leave without having enough time to plan for post resignation. I had taken a huge risk. I have to own that decision, think ahead, and move forward.

> I have to own that decision, think ahead, and move forward.

But at forty, 'forward' was a tricky word. I do have a relatively long experience, but what kind of experience?

That was the question. The financial package did solve some pressing needs, such as paying off some loans and preparing to build or buy a house for my family. But that wasn't enough to diminish the bubbling question marks in front of my folks' faces: "Now what? What's your plan, Mohamed? You have no job and no fixed source of income." I couldn't blame them.

> But at forty, 'forward' was a tricky word.

My Life On A Piece Of Paper

My Curriculum Vitae (CV) in 2010, was totally different from the one I had submitted in1993 when I had applied for my first job. It was far messier and more muddled. It said everything about me except that I had a consistent career path with a conscious and intentional advancement. None of the lanes I had taken were long or steady enough to impress recruiters.

'Frankenstein' was perhaps the best description of my CV. No segment of it was uniform enough to get me back into work uniform again. A huge and creative effort was needed to rewrite the CV in a way that I could present myself and my competence persuasively and professionally. Still, any employer would notice, either in the CV or later in the interview, that I was not good enough.

Who Am I?

The employers' potential impressions were one thing, and my immediate self-perception was another. Who am I really? An electrical engineering graduate? A power generation technical operator? A Safety Practitioner? A public speaker? An industrial professional?

I didn't ask these questions when I was on the job. I guess my job was the thread that held all these marbles together. My recent position as the safety superintendent was solid enough to conceal all the inconsistencies and incongruities that made up my professional life. And when that job— that 'thread'— got cut, all the pieces fell down, scattering and shattering how I viewed myself.

I needed to pick myself up. But first, I needed to pick these scattered pieces of myself. The question was: "Which ones?" Which pieces should I pick and which ones should I leave? Now that they were all spread out and I could see them in detail, I had a choice in redefining who I was. So, what were my options?

Pick electrical engineering. No, occupational safety. No, power generation. No, public speaking is better. The problem was that picking any one meant discarding all the others.

Ok, let me take all of them, and leave nothing out. Wait, then I would be all things for everyone. That's not a good deal, and no deal can come from this choice.

> I needed to pick myself up. But first, I needed to pick these scattered pieces of myself.

What if I leave everything as it is and start something new? But what is it going to be? And at forty, how long would it take me to master and perfect a new profession?

Who's To Blame?

My father? He was the one who put me on an academic path (electrical engineering) that I was not interested in. But then, he just wanted the best for me at the time.

My Creator? But He's not the one who forced me into paths and plans that ended up being incoherent, to say the least.

Myself? It has to come back to me, doesn't it? Even if I claim that many key decisions were not taken by me but for me, I willingly followed through and continued on whatever path they led me to.

It's Not Their Fault: Family

Why should they suffer? Why should they be the victims of a poorly thought-out decision? Although, deep inside, I was pretty sure I had made the right choice at that time.

I simply couldn't explain or justify my decision to them, no matter how hard I tried.

They stopped trying to change my mind. They loved me and trusted me. Moreover, they knew that no further amount of pressure would cause me to reverse my decision, they just surrendered to my will. We continued life as best as we could.

This didn't soften the harsh reality of an unclear future plan to support them with a decent career once again. Following your heart can be the wisest thing to do at a certain point. But it's the heart that aches the most when loved ones are the ones most affected by listening to it. To put it simply, the heart tells you to do what hurts it.

> To put it simply, the heart tells you to do what hurts it.

Nobody In The Middle Of Nowhere

There I stood, reflecting on 33 years (of studying and working)—dozens of certificates and qualifications accumulated over the years.

Mountains of experiences, events, and exposures. Heaps of knowledge and education. Hoards of achievements, accolades and accomplishments. Piles of hopes, dreams and ambitions. A career shredded into bales of dry leaves.

A Life Torn Into Pieces

Before I left the company, everything seemed logical. I was a bag of skin holding everything tightly. I was a collection of many skills and strengths under one name. It all made sense. However, just by removing the job, title, and company badge, suddenly, everything became senseless. I could no longer put the parts of me – which were essentially me – together again.

I was in the middle of my life; nobody in the middle of nowhere.

Then, one day, I opened my email inbox.

> I was in the middle of my life; nobody in the middle of nowhere.

***

"This program was a turning point in my career. One of the biggest lessons is that no one copies what I do or what I am good at; because no one has my knowledge and experience. Whoever applies this principle will gain real distinction, and not just another number"

– Dr. Thuraya Juma
University Professor, Bahrain

*** *** ***

Take A Moment And Think:

- Have you ever found yourself having to make yet another unexpected career choice in the middle of your career?
- Was it easier or harder than the choices you made at the start of your career?
- Have you had to switch careers, migrate from one to another, or remain in one and let opportunities pass?
- Have you ever been stuck in an 'either or' mindset regarding career progression, where every choice meant winning something and losing everything else, including your expertise, talents, and competencies?
- Do you consider uncertainty a place that hides threat, insecurity and loss for you; or a place that holds opportunity, possibilities, and gains?

Your thoughts here:

*** *** ***

PART 2

Saudi Arabia: A Big Yes To Living Big

CHAPTER 5

THE PROJECT

Come To Saudi Arabia

That was the gist of the email I opened. The summer of 2012 was nearly over. More than two years had passed since I left my company. I didn't have a job nor was I seeking one. Yet, this email was inviting me to join one of the region's biggest power companies as a consultant, for a two-year 'Safety Project'.

The sender briefly explained that my role would primarily involve conducting safety training for supervisors and middle managers across the company. It was part of a broader company-wide initiative aimed at boosting safety performance by upgrading the safety system, improving compliance, and enhancing the overall safety culture.

That's strange! I did not remember applying to any company, nor had I posted my CV anywhere (remember my wobbly 'Frankenstein' CV?). Besides, who said I was a consultant? I never claimed to be one, and I certainly never imagined I could be.

The email, though, looked genuine and authentic.

Thanks! But No Thanks!

That – basically – was my reply. Why? Because the idea of being away from my family for a whole two years was just too daunting. I couldn't leave my wife and children for such a long time. Even if I could visit them every now and then, a big part of me refused the whole idea.

Maybe it was because I had never done freelance work before, especially abroad. I was used to having a day job, not far from where I lived, and spending the rest of the day with my family. This offer, however, was suggesting that I'd be far from home for extended periods. I might manage the workload and stay busy with my new assignment, but what about my family? How would they cope? I knew my father and mother weren't comfortable with it. My family was used to me being close and available.

So, my answer was a straight "Sorry! Thank you, but no thank you!"

I declined the offer.

Sorry, But No Sorrys

They just didn't take 'no' for an answer. They asked for the reasons behind my rejection (so that they could find solutions).

"Too long? We will create a customized schedule that suits you!"

"Too far from your family for too long? We're ready to grant you extra air tickets so you can fly back to Bahrain and see them every fortnight!"

I felt like an 'overbooked celebrity' whose availability was nearly impossible. Except that I had no other work commitments, nor was I acting in such a way to create a deeper sense of demand from the client. I wasn't attempting to raise their temptation—or, consequently, my pay. I hadn't negotiated anything; I just felt I wasn't ready for this kind of work commitment.

A 'Tug Of War' Game

The company representative just wouldn't give up. He was pulling from his end, and I was pulling from mine. This tug-of-war went on for weeks, mostly through emails and occasionally through phone calls. During those communications, I also learned more about the project and its context. Furthermore, I became more curious about the nature of freelancing work as I discussed the matter with friends who were in the business.

All that, however, did little to bring us— the client and me—closer to an agreement. More events arose as further excuses for me to reject the offer. I started to receive a few requests to conduct short-duration safety courses in my country, Bahrain. This way, I could begin some work here without having to travel. My father's health condition needed more attention, and being away from him (as the eldest son) wasn't a good idea.

Did the client let go of the rope? You guessed it: no.

They made what seemed like their last attempt.

***

"As a Speaker and workshop Facilitator, I have been fortunate to conduct, and to participate in events around the world, to listen and learn from some of the best presenters, and non better than 'The One And Only' workshop given by Mohamed Shukri, in Colombo, Sri Lanka in 2018. The workshop was brilliantly different, in acknowledging that each of us has the unique potential to become a 'champion' at what we do, and I quickly took on board all that I learned, from 'The One And Only' workshop, strengthened my resolve, to discover my niche, take action, and deliver my keynotes and workshops."

– David Hughes
Writer & Speaker, Australia

*** *** ***

Take A Moment And Think:

- Have you ever been offered a job or a position before? Where and when was it? Was it internal in your company or external by another company?
- How did that compare with you chasing and applying for jobs? Are they the same?
- Wasn't the sense of being needed and valued fulfilling, regardless of how fulfilling the offer was?
- What do all those who are sought after or headhunted have in common? Can you see a pattern? Do you have what makes you sought after as a professional? What is it, or rather what are *they?*
- Have you tried to learn what organizations may need from you, rather than focusing on what you need from them?

Your thoughts here:

*** *** ***

CHAPTER 6

WHY ME?

The Call

It was February 2013. Almost three months of communication with the client had gone by, with neither of us willing to give in to the other. Until then, I was completely in the dark regarding the client's attempts to secure another consultant or consultants.

Who knew? Who cared? I didn't. My decision was firm. Why should they care, too? They were a large organization and had access to as many experts and consultants as they wanted; there were myriads of them out there.

They did care, though. At least, that was what I sensed in the frequency and tone of their communication. They actually arranged a phone call to discuss the matter with me. Strangely, I agreed to have the conversation.

The caller was the head safety consultant for the entire project at the power company. As safety practitioners, we bonded quickly, and he went on to give an overall view of the project and my expected role in it, which was mainly delivering 'Safety Supervisory' training to approximately one thousand supervisors and middle managers.

Okay, You Got My Attention

"That's it?" I thought. There was no reason they had hunted me down all these weeks just to perform this task. But the mere fact that they decided to have a call, despite my repetitive rejections previously, caught my attention and made me curious. Despite the abundance of candidates who could perfectly fit this requirement, why were they hunting me down in particular?

So, I did what anyone in my place would do and asked the person on the other end the obvious and unavoidable question:

- "Why me? You do realize you have so many options, sir, don't you?"
- "Oh, yes, we do. But we started with you, and we're keen on having you, if we can."
- "Why? Why me?"
- "Well, for one, electricity is our company's business, and we know that you are an Electrical Engineer, to start with."

Where did they get that piece of information from? I haven't posted my CV anywhere! However, I replied:

- "That only?"
- "That, and the other thing is the fact that you have worked in power generation for at least 10 years. This is a key factor for us, as we are in the power generation business."

Right! So, they knew more about me than I thought they have. And although the project was a 'safety' project and required none of my electrical or power generation expertise, they saw these two background elements as plus points.

I continued, though, unconvinced I was the rarest option, let alone the sole option. I demanded more compelling reasons:

- "Hmmm! What else?"
- "You see, Mr. Mohamed, we are launching a new safety management system. We have to get the middle management's buy-in on the already approved system by top management. And we know that you are an expert on the system, which is the 'SMS system'."

"What?!" I exclaimed internally. The same little program I was assigned to master and implement in my previous company 9 years ago?! The system I never thought anyone outside my then company would adopt. The system I became an accredited auditor for, but thought would stay idle and orphaned on my CV for the rest of my life. The system no one would ever be interested in or in hiring me because of it. And now, these guys are calling me for my knowledge of this exact system!

Aha!

This meant that I had another counter-attack, a staggering excuse to reject their request; and this time for good. Since this was their selling point to win me over, I thought, let me flip it back to him!:

- "Sir, I understand and appreciate that. Since you mentioned this, allow me to suggest an alternative—29 alternatives, in fact."
- "Go ahead!"
- "To give you some background, Mr. '……', I know 29 other safety practitioners who are also eligible and accredited auditors on this system. I can get you their names and contacts, and you can select and invite any of them."
- "We know them all."
- "Excuse me?!"
- "I said, we know who you are talking about, and we have their contacts."
- "And…?!"
- "And… we decided we want you."

Running Out Of Excuses

I was truly taken aback and felt trapped. I thought that I had finally found a way out, and it was time to call it a day. I believed I had totally disarmed him. He had 29 other candidates to select from and could have avoided wasting his time with me for at least three months. Why were they insisting on hiring me and not one of them? I asked that question once and for the last time.

I thought, "He'd better give me a good reason!"

- "Why me?!"
- "Good question. Why you and not your expert colleagues? This one is a bit more complicated. But in short, getting the buy-in from a critical layer of the organization (i.e., the middle management), who would be directly responsible for the implementation of the system, is a heavy challenge. Therefore, it is not enough for us to enlist someone who is merely an expert and knowledgeable about the system. While that is an important feature, we are looking for additional and specific abilities that will ensure our employees are not only informed and educated about the new system but also convinced and committed. And we have another piece of information about you that serves this purpose."

- "Yeah, and what is that?"

- "We know that you have a solid reputation for delivering safety workshops, courses, presentations, and papers in a rather compelling and inspiring manner. Weren't you the 'World Championship of Public Speaking' finalist in 2006 in Washington, DC?"
- "Yes, I was!"
- "So? If you were in my place, leading a tough task to get maximum consensus and collaboration for a key organizational system migration, would you select an alternative that is less likely to create the impact you need to see positive results? As a safety practitioner, you have the ability to both educate and motivate audiences when you address and speak to them. I hope it's clear now why we tracked you down all the way. We have to do our best to get what – and who – is best for this particular assignment. And you are the best one for this job, Mohamed - if not the only one. So, what do you say?"

You Win!

"Yes!" I said. "Yes, I will take the job!"

***

"Reshaping my perspective on my life, this enlightening workshop encouraged me to appreciate my uniqueness, recognizing that my diverse skills contribute to a larger purpose, transforming me from an Assistant Manager to a General Manager today as I approach each day with confidence that I can truly make a difference as 'The One And Only'."

– Zaidh Naushard
General Manager, Strategic Business Development APAC, Sri Lanka

*** *** ***

Take A Moment And Think:

- Have you considered that the skills and knowledge from past jobs stay with you, even after you leave?
- If so, wouldn't it make more sense to keep all of your expertise accessible in case a need or opportunity arises, rather than disregarding it as though it never happened?
- When organizations show interest, is it typically for one specific skill or a combination of your talents and attributes?
- What are some of your strongest <u>individual</u> skills?
- Which of your skills are only average when used alone, yet when combined are strong?

Your thoughts here:

*** *** ***

CHAPTER 7

TRASH TO TREASURE

Nothing Was A Waste

Everything had worth—high worth. The education I once despised, the job I endured, the certifications I downplayed, and the skills I deemed obsolete—every single one of them was valuable. But together, they made me the preferred option for this particular project.

I had dumped all of them in the trash bin of time. Yet now, someone was interested in that trash. The funniest part was that no single piece was wanted on its own. All the features mentioned by the client in response to my 'Why me?' pressing queries were valuable only when combined, not separately. It was like a jigsaw puzzle, where the full picture is revealed only when all the pieces are arranged in the right way. Until then, the pieces remained meaningless, the picture incomplete, and my life a puzzle.

My CV: from Beast To Beauty

Overnight, my ugly Frankenstein CV turned into a beauty. I hadn't changed anything in its content or ingredients. Following the phone conversation and the client's request to send an 'updated' version of my CV, I reopened it, only to see it in a totally new light. Suddenly, the mundane bullet points listing my experience and qualifications transformed into glowing, golden lines.

It's true that the client's specific needs made my CV turn from beast to beauty. However, I cannot underestimate the paradigm shift in how I now viewed my past. And guess what? There was no evidence this applied strictly and only to the current client—the Saudi company.

From Contradicting To Contributing

What kind of coincidence was this? It made me realize that my seemingly conflicting past life events had actually aligned and conspired in my favor.

My upset-about an inconsistent and messy career-turned into an uplift. By just looking at it from a different angle, I witnessed how the mess could become a solid and strong mass.

Do you recall any painting that mesmerized you at first sight? It is nothing more than a messy canvas full of splashed colors, if you choose to look at it that way. Take a deeper, more detailed look at every square centimeter of the painting. Focus on that spot alone for a minute, separate from all the other parts. What do you see? Nothing that's worth looking at, let alone hanging in a gallery. And if you happen to visit the artist in his studio while he is in the middle of creating his work, all you will see is a mess.

The artist doesn't see it that way, though. Every line he draws, every curve he makes, and every color he chooses has value. He is patient and confident about how all this will end up. You, on the other hand, would be impatient. You would soon leave the studio, uninterested in what he's crafting, finding it all too boring and meaningless to watch. But at the right time, both of you will celebrate the work—how all the pieces came together to create a brilliant and beautiful masterpiece.

It's all about timing.

All In One And One For All

In my case with the Saudi company, timing—and the context of the required service—were crucial. The messy and seemingly meaningless splash of colors I saw in my career and experience was, for the client, the perfect portrait. From my standpoint, my chaotic career fit nowhere; from his perspective, it was the missing piece of art for a new villa. Maybe if we both stood in front of the painting (my profile) from the same angle, we wouldn't be impressed by it. However, in the context of the company's urgent need for a particular task and solution, my career was worth acquiring and positioning within its transitional strategy, at the very least.

This meant that even my 'masterpiece' wasn't truly a masterpiece until it was placed within the bigger picture: the client's specific challenge and need. It's not enough to piece my life together in any shape or form, and simply wish it would transform into a brilliant painting – that would be an actual splash of color. My 'masterpiece' must be connected to another picture to become a larger and more meaningful work of art.

ALL the pieces the client looked for were found in ONE piece: me. This ONE piece became ALL what the client wanted.

All in one and one for all.

> ALL the pieces the client looked for were found in ONE piece: me. This ONE piece became ALL what the client wanted.
> All in one and one for all.

One Last Request

The hunt came to an end, and I surrendered. I decided to take on the project. Strangely, the reasons why I had declined it at the beginning of the chase hadn't changed.

I still found it a challenging mission to work away from my family for such a long time. However, the client did loosen the terms of engagement by the time we reached this stage of discussion.

My level of engagement was redefined in both quantity and quality. I no longer had to report for a daily duty period and perform a long list of tasks as a full-time consultant. Instead, my role was focused primarily on the main reason they wanted me as a consultant: training. They organized a schedule that helped them achieve just that: intensive training for the target supervisors and managers, with an emphasis on motivation, inspiration, and buy-in that I had to secure in each and every session.

Yet, something came up, and I had to make one last request to the client: "Can we start in May or June instead of April 2013?" I explained the reason, which he acknowledged. My father's health had been slowly deteriorating over the past few years, and his memory was diminishing even faster. During the months I was in discussion with the client, my father 'announced' that he was planning to travel to Mumbai, India. We all knew he couldn't travel alone. We tried to dissuade him from the idea and somewhat hoped he would wake up the next morning having forgotten he ever wanted to travel.

He didn't!

He kept insisting until we finally gave in. We arranged to take him to Mumbai in April.

***

"'The One and Only' program was truly inspiring. The insights provided a fresh perspective that helped spark the creation of my bestselling collaborative book 'The Green PMO'"

– Eman Deabil
Management Consultant, Bahrain

*** *** ***

Take A Moment And Think:

- Looking back, are there 'wastes' — things, events, or choices you regret and wish hadn't happened in your life?
- If you opened up about these 'wastes' to a close and sincere friend, how do you think they would respond?
- Would you be the same person reading these lines if those events hadn't happened? Would you still have the same clarity, wisdom, and experience?
- Review your CV or an updated version of your skills and experiences. If you were a recruiter at 'ABC' company, how would you view it? What talents would catch your interest? What strengths would you want to invest in?
- Grab a pen or a marker and use a printed copy of your CV to draw patterns and lines connecting your skills and strengths. Be creative—connect skills, competencies, and talents that don't match, won't fit, or are even opposites, and see what you come up with.
- Explore various industries and markets to identify how your 'combinations' can form a new niche. Continuously navigate between your professional past and the current job market, and you'll be surprised by the countless possibilities and opportunities you can uncover.

Your thoughts here:

*** *** ***

PART 3

Mumbai & Mangalore: Miracles

CHAPTER 8

FROM MANAMA TO MUMBAI

Dad's Desire And Disease

On a rainy night, I received a call that my dad had gone through a terrible experience. As he walked his last steps toward where his friends had gathered, he slipped and fell into one of the water puddles. He was heavily drenched and in a mess, but more severely affected on an emotional level. My youngest brother took him home, helped him take a shower, and got him to sleep.

When he woke up in the morning, he made an announcement: "I am going to Mumbai," he told my mother. Dad's memory had been in a slow but steady decline over the past couple of years. Therefore, my mother took that as another 'fantasy' and hoped he would forget this one as well. He didn't forget; rather, he repeated his intention again and again, and his determination grew stronger day by day.

Our mother informed me and my siblings of our dad's deepening desire to travel once again to his old and never-dying favorite destination: Mumbai. We all knew that his physical and mental fitness did not allow him to travel on his own, something he kept denying while defying attempts to talk him out of the idea. Of course, he couldn't. Although he remembered very well his undying love for the place where his life was saved when he was young.

In his youth, he was afflicted with a lung disease and had undergone surgery in India, after which he lived healthily. He also took us—his family—to India several times to enjoy some of his vacations. His memories of India were too vivid to fade away, even though he was showing signs of what appeared to be Alzheimer's.

We had no choice but to ignore his incessant requests. He had shown unmistakable signs of amnesia and forgetfulness. In fact, his recent incident of falling into the puddle was due to some of those symptoms: gait problems (limping every 3–4 steps). He would often forget his way home while driving and would call us to pick him up or show him how to get back. He would look for his daughter by calling her name, even though she was sitting right in front of him.

Looking at all these signs separately, we attributed them to the advancement of age—not to mention his existing chronic diseases like diabetes and hypertension. However, there came a point when the entire family reached a concrete conclusion: dad had Alzheimer's. There was no way he didn't. After observing those who suffered from Alzheimer's around us and confirming it with medical information, we had to surrender to the fact that my father was inevitably ill with this incurable brain disorder.

As you can see, we had every reason not to give in to dad's delusional desire to travel to India. Even if we accompanied him, how comfortable and enjoyable would the trip be for him, given his current health condition? What made us confident that dad was merely fantasizing—as he often did—was his constant refrain: "I want to travel to India. I want to meet my friend Sagar." You see, Sagar was an old colleague of dad's who had returned to his home country, India, many years ago. In fact, dad mentioned Sagar right after waking up from that dreadful night. This convinced us that it was just a dream he had, and when he woke up, he began describing what was clearly a delusion. This random recollection of Sagar in his sleep was definitely a good excuse for us to downplay his dream and distract him from his decision.

Flying To Mumbai

But this was dad—my determined, hard-hitting, go-getter dad—who was our model for making things happen and getting things done. He had raised us with immense compassion and care, like every fighting father does. He fostered not only his direct children but also almost every member of the broader family, who were grateful for his unconditional and generous touch in any aspect of their lives you could imagine.

Perhaps that's why, when his youngest brother (my uncle) picked up the phone one day and called me, I deferred to dad's will and wish. My uncle, in his usual sharp tone mixed with emotional warmth, told me, "Why don't you just take your dad to India? He loves India and Mumbai. Take him. As long as he has some memory and can identify you as his children, take him and let him enjoy the trip with his loved ones. What's wrong with that?!"

My younger brother and I took our mother's blessings and started planning to take our father to Mumbai. Our loving mother equipped us with everything we needed to take good care of her lifelong partner and better half.

April 2013 was around the corner, and everything was set. Our visas were ready, and my brother had taken a leave from his work. I didn't have a day job, but I did have an upcoming project with the Saudi company. I had that company delay my engagement by another month so that I could be with my father and brother on this important trip.

Before we left, our mother, a diligent and organized wife and mother, made sure we hadn't overlooked anything.

She astonished me with her meticulous attention to detail. She didn't leave any aspect untouched. Neither did she fail to foresee any issues that could potentially occur during our trip. Who knew my dad better than her, anyway?

No wonder she proposed one more thing: "While you're there, take your father for a medical checkup," she asked us, her two sons. "A regular but thorough medical check is a good investment of your time. When it comes to healthcare, India has made a significant impact on your dad's well-being in his youth." So, the medical checkup was added to our plan.

In Mumbai

Dad enjoyed every day in Mumbai. Luckily, he completely forgot about meeting his friend Sagar. We had no information about his whereabouts, nor had we had any connection with him since he left Bahrain nearly two decades ago. Our daily routine consisted of touring Mumbai's sightseeing spots. We took him to Gandhi's house and museum, visited 'The Taj' one of Mumbai's biggest attractions and considered one of the finest hotels in India. The Gateway of India was another stop where dad loved taking photos. Colaba Road became dad's favorite go-to place. The markets were particularly appealing to me, with their flamboyant fabrics and glittery golden accessories that were must-haves for my wife and two young daughters. Every now and then, we stopped to drink fresh coconut water, which was a cool and casual treat. Dad was the best tour guide we could have.

He told us tales about how Mumbai had changed over the years. I can't recall the number of times he visited the city, but I could tell how dear it was to his heart from the way he felt and behaved while we were there. It wasn't too difficult, however, to recall scenes from when dad had brought us to Mumbai during our childhood.

Earlier in his life, he had worked in an air fueling company as the superintendent of operations. I'm not sure how many free or discounted air tickets he received as part of his employment incentives (if there were any, for that matter). Regardless, he took my mother and us children to India, particularly to Mumbai, several times.

The irony wasn't hard to miss, though. There he was now, after all these years, being flown to India by his two grown-up boys—whom he had once protected, carried in his strong arms, and taken around this very city. Today, we were taking care of him in the same city. His weak body could barely move, but his heart remained strong and full of love for us and for this astonishing place.

We still had one task to complete before heading back home: dad's medical checkup. My brother had everything planned in advance. As soon as we landed in Mumbai, he arranged for a doctor to visit dad in his hotel room. In fact, he managed to get two reputable doctors to examine him. Both doctors reviewed dad's symptoms, prescribed several tests, and recommended a couple of hospitals and medical labs for further evaluation.

An Unexpected Discovery

After all the medical tests were completed, we scheduled an appointment with Dr. Omar at one of Mumbai's renowned hospitals. Dr. Omar reviewed the test results and recommended a few more tests, including an fMRI[4]. Although this wasn't part of our initial plan for 'regular checkups' there was no reason to decline. We had come too far, both in distance and in medical evaluations, so we decided not to skip this one last test.

After the test, the three of us—my brother, father, and I—visited Dr. Omar at his clinic to hear his opinion on dad's reports. Dr. Omar, a neurosurgeon, had shown great support and deep respect for our father throughout the process. That evening, we sat outside his office, waiting for our turn to be called in. I could sense that my brother and I were silently grappling with the uncertainty of what the recent test might reveal about dad's condition.

What more could Dr. Omar, a neurosurgeon, add to what we already knew? We were well aware that dad

---

[4] fMRI: Abbreviation for Functional MRI. MRI stands for Magnetic Resonance Imaging. This is a type of body scan.

was suffering from Alzheimer's, and the symptoms were steadily worsening.

"Ali Shukri!" The nurse called, signaling that it was our turn to see the doctor. We guided our dad, who was using his walking stick, into the room. Dr Omar stood up to personally welcome him and walk him to his seat. However, my father didn't walk directly to his chair. After shaking Dr Omar's hand, he paused for a moment, glanced around the small room, and then, rested his eyes on the doctor. He said in a calm and friendly voice: "Doctor, I feel healing in your room!"

What did dad just say? What exactly did he really feel? As much as I wanted to know the answer, his words took both of us by surprise. But the moment and the situation forced us to move on, dismissing dad's strange comment as one of the random bits of wisdom he would sometimes throw. Dr Omar responded with a gentle smile. We all sat down, bracing for what felt like a verdict. Dr Omar didn't make us wait long.

"Your father doesn't have Alzheimer's!"

A Difficult Decision

"What!" My brother and I were in shock. I split my stunned gaze between Dr Omar's firm yet friendly face and my dad, who sat a meter away from us. He appeared calm, looking at us with curiosity. However, he wasn't following the discussion, partly because he couldn't focus on conversations he wasn't directly part of. We had also made a conscious effort to keep our voices low, ensuring dad wouldn't hear every detail about his condition.

"How come?" I exclaimed softly. "All dad's symptoms say otherwise!" Dr Omar replied, "The symptoms you observe in your father are very similar to another syndrome called 'NPH[5]'—Normal Pressure Hydrocephalus." He continued to explain the disease in simple terms, emphasizing that when NPH is caught early, its effects can be reversed by a procedure called ventricular shunting[6], which he recommended for dad. He assured us that dad's condition was curable and that surgery was the only way forward.

We were drenched in mixed feelings. While we were relieved that our father didn't have Alzheimer's, an incurable and irreversible disease, we were unsure if he could really undergo surgery at his age, considering all the other chronic conditions he had.

Dr Omar explained the nature of the surgery and assured us that our father was fit for it, advising us not to worry at all. He had performed many ventricular shunting surgeries, and his clarity and confidence only added to our

---

[5] NPH: Normal Pressure Hydrocephalus.
[6] Ventricular shunting: It is a surgical procedure that treats hydrocephalus, a condition where there is too much cerebrospinal fluid (CSF) in the brain and spinal cord.

reassurance. He even suggested that we could schedule the surgery within three days, as we needed to travel back to Bahrain in a few days.

We returned to our hotel room. "Three days? Here in Mumbai?" My brother and I couldn't sleep that night. We needed to decide and act fast. We hadn't heard of this disease before, so my brother conducted extensive research online and gathered a substantial amount of information. We learned about our dad's condition in record time. Still, we were not experts, and we had only listened to one doctor. Seeking a second opinion was the least we could do for our dear father. As reassuring as Dr Omar's words were, our father's health and life were the most precious things to us at that moment.

Shall we go ahead with the surgery? Should we return to Bahrain and decide later? What if we go back and delay his treatment to the point where his syndrome cannot be reversed? What if we do it here and now? What if something goes wrong due to his age and other health conditions? Is there another way we can be more certain? Is there anyone we can reach out to here?

My brother and I called our mother and siblings, ensuring that dad was unaware of any of these discussions. We had to grapple with the dilemma of our lives; any option we chose would have significant consequences. I wished there was someone who could tell us what to do or at least offer a piece of advice or direction. But we didn't know anyone in this country well enough to provide that valuable guidance.

"Wait a minute!" My brother suddenly exclaimed. "But we do! I know someone, and I will contact him immediately."

***

"After attending Mohamed Shukri's 'The One And Only' program, I was left with an unforgettable experience. The program fundamentally shifted my perspective, moving my focus away from seeking significance and success in any field toward developing my unique skills and experiences. By honing these skills, I aim to create a distinctive niche that sets me apart from others. This approach eliminated the need for frantic competition and allowed me to engage in a more balanced and self-paced journey toward personal growth."

– Doha Melato
Pharmacist, supply chain officer,
life coach, Saudi Arabia

*** *** ***

Take A Moment And Think:

- Imagine your 80-year-old self is having a conversation with your 20 or 30-year-old self. How would that conversation go?
- What is your older version saying to your younger version?
- What is your younger version saying to your older version?
- What do you wish you had done at a younger age to benefit your older self?
- At 80, what do you think you would regret having done more, and what would you regret having done less? Make a list of both, and regardless of your current age or stage in life, start living a new life.

Your thoughts here:

*** ******

CHAPTER 9

MIRACLES IN MANGALORE

From Mumbai To Mangalore

Did I mention that my brother was working at the same air fueling company our father retired from? We were unsure whose help to seek in India. That's when my brother suddenly remembered Sagar.

"Sagar!" I exclaimed. "You don't mean Sagar, our dad's former colleague, do you? The one our father thought he saw in his vision a couple of months ago and insisted on flying to India to meet?"

"Yes, that's him, Mohamed!"

"But how on earth are we going to reach him? We don't have his contact number, nor do we know where he lives!"

"I have his email address. In fact, I already emailed him, and he responded. He lives in Mangalore!" That was my proactive brother, as usual.

"Great! And…?"

"He asked me to send dad's medical reports, which I've already done. Now, we're just waiting for his response!"

I remembered Sagar very well. I, too, had worked at my dad's company, though only during my summer vocational training in college. Even though my dad was in operations and Sagar was in maintenance, it was easy to see how close they were. Whenever I was around, Sagar never missed an opportunity to give me special attention. He would teach me basic maintenance concepts, chat with me—knowing I was eager to improve my English—or simply share jokes with me and dad during our coffee breaks.

It wasn't long before Sagar responded. Finally, we received some helpful guidance regarding the next step in dad's treatment. What we got, however, was much more than just guidance. Sagar informed my brother that he had a cousin who was also a neurosurgeon. After reviewing dad's reports, Dr Sahil Bantwal, Sagar's cousin, confirmed Dr Omar's diagnosis and the recommendation for surgery.

This news provided the second opinion we had been seeking, bringing us a sense of relief despite the looming decision ahead. That wasn't all—Sagar proposed we fly to Mangalore, where he was living, and have our father undergo surgery at one of the local healthcare facilities. He mentioned that Dr Sahil, who happened to be a visiting specialist at Unity Hospital, would be more than happy to perform the surgery for Ali, his old colleague and friend.

Sagar's suggestion offered not only medical reassurance but also the comfort of a familiar connection, making the decision feel a little less daunting.

Dr Sahil's expertise and reputation in the field of neurosurgery went beyond India's borders, and he was one of the country's top neurosurgeons at that time. Sagar left us with no choice, pulling us out of our dilemma by presenting compelling reasons to fly our dad to Mangalore. He assured us that our father would receive the finest, most reliable, and even affordable treatment—especially for what could be the most critical and decisive health-related action in dad's life.

We informed our dad, briefed our mother, got everyone's consensus, and quickly began planning for the new trip. My brother rescheduled our flights so that we could stay in India long enough to complete the treatment, and he booked the earliest domestic flight from Mumbai to Mangalore.

Meeting Sagar

We landed in Mangalore and we finally met Sagar. The two old friends and colleagues, my father and Sagar, reunited after a very long time, with pure elation and joy, reliving memories of the past. It felt surreal—was this a dream, or had a dream truly come to life? Dad's dream had come true, and now I was living what was truly a dream. Even when we planned the trip to fulfill part of his wish, meeting Sagar was never part of the expectation. Yet, here we were, witnessing a reunion we had never fully believed possible.

But now, unknowingly, we had literally fulfilled his wish—every part of it. How was this even possible? The more I reflect on it, even to this day, the more perplexed I become. There had been no plan, no scheme, not even the slightest intention to bring every detail of my father's dream to life. When we agreed to take him to India, my father had completely forgotten about Sagar, especially as the departure date from Bahrain approached. He was simply preoccupied, and happy with the idea that he was traveling to Mumbai. That was enough for him—or so we thought. Yet, somehow, every element of his wish had aligned, effortlessly falling into place, as if it were meant to be.

> Yet, somehow, every element of his wish had aligned, effortlessly falling into place, as if it were meant to be.

Here we were, in Mangalore, meeting Sagar, the man of my father's dream—who was now real, tangible, and standing before us. The flood of mixed emotions overwhelmed us all. Joy, relief, and gratitude filled the air, leaving us little room to question how everything had come together so perfectly, and in just two weeks.

Yet, we had a mission to complete. The last piece of this puzzling trip was still to be placed. We still needed to prepare dad for the surgery, both physically and mentally. Sagar had everything arranged with his cousin, Dr Sahil, and Unity Hospital.

A Medical Miracle?

In his bed at Unity Hospital my father was well taken care of by every staff member. He spent around two days undergoing pre-surgery checkups. "He's good to go," Dr Bantwal reassured us.

The night before the surgery, my father was nervous.

He asked, with an anxious look on his face, "Mohamed, can you place a call to your mother? I want to speak to her!"

We gave him the phone, and he started talking to her in a broken voice. We only recognized the first few words—our mother's name, the greetings—and then nothing. His voice, mixed with tears, touched us deeply. When he started sobbing, we moved away from his chair so he wouldn't see us and we wouldn't hear him. We were just respecting his privacy and dignity.

I don't remember seeing dad this weak before. After all, he was the one we leaned on whenever we were weak or ill. He took each one of us, including my mother, countless times to medical centers and hospitals, both in Bahrain and abroad, bearing all the expenses and costs. Witnessing the flip side of dad's life was too painful to bear. All my life, I saw dad as the lion who took good care of his kingdom and his kids.

My pain was interrupted, though, when dad hung up the call with our mother. He looked relieved and relaxed. What happened? What did mom tell him that turned his distress 180 degrees into almost delight? Or was it the calmness that came from the mere conversation with his life partner? Whatever it was, dad looked at us and, without a word, said, "I am ready."

The surgery was over, and dad was out of the theater. Dr Bantwal informed us that the operation was a 100% success. The following day, dad was in good condition. When we asked him, "How was the operation?" he replied, "What operation?" Oh no! Did he forget again? Was the dementia still there and strong? Just before we adopted that conclusion, dad smiled and said, "The operation was so light; I didn't even feel I had one."

Okay. It was dad again, saying things in the funniest way he could. Even though his head was covered with bandages and stitches, he bloomed like never before.

The doctors said he would need to be extra careful when moving and would still need his walking stick to move around for at least the next two days.

On day three, everything changed. The only time we had to keep him in the wheelchair was to go to the reception desk of Unity Hospital, where we were completing his discharge formalities. At the desk, however, dad stood up, walked to the entrance door, and before he stepped out, my brother (who was waiting outside with his camera) shouted, "Dad, throw your stick!" Dad was ready for this; he did exactly that and walked like the lion we always saw and knew, wearing a big victory smile. We laughed as we captured that moment on camera.

Was this really happening? Only two weeks ago, dad's condition seemed hopeless. All signs pointed to an inevitably increasing and irreversible progression of Alzheimer's symptoms, taking every conscious piece of dad's well-being for the rest of his life. The man we are looking at now is a totally different person. He doesn't limp anymore and needs no canes or wheelchairs to move. In 72 hours of careful observation, my brother and I couldn't catch him displaying any signs of dementia. He was fresh, strong, and full of joy. All other symptoms diminished rapidly. The doctors in Mumbai and Mangalore told us these symptoms would disappear soon after the operation, and they did.

It was nothing short of a medical miracle. Even if the doctors viewed it as a normal procedure, which they kept stressing over and over, for us, who have gone through the entire journey from desperation to salvation, it was a miracle. A miracle in more than just one aspect.

The Real Miracle(s)

The puzzle was solved. All pieces were rightly and brilliantly placed. The big picture was crystal clear. I'd like to think of dad's dream as nothing more than a coincidence that led us to eventually give in to his insistence. But when I connect all the events—from that dark and soaking night he went through to this point—I can see nothing but a perfect plan. Except that we didn't plan, expect, or even dream of this—not even any part of it. None of us did: my brother, my father, my mother, Sagar, or anyone else. And yet, it now looks perfectly designed, every single piece of it.

Everything in our trip had unfolded in mysterious ways. All the seemingly conflicting, scattered pieces of events have finally revealed themselves as parts of one solid and brilliant work. Everything conspired in dad's best interest, without him, us, or anyone else being involved.

That terrible rainy night—dad falling into the puddle, waking up the next day demanding to travel to India and meet 'Sagar', my uncle's call urging that his brother's wish be granted, my mother's blessing and specific request for us to get her husband medical checkups, Dr Omar's unexpected finding that dad had no Alzheimer's, finding Sagar, and traveling to Mangalore—all these pieces seemed awkward and irrelevant when viewed separately.

But now, here in Mangalore, everything made total sense. Before we departed, I had grasped the magnificence of more than one miracle.

> I had grasped the magnificence of more than one miracle.

The 'One And Only' Sagar

At the beginning of our arrival in Mangalore, I had asked Sagar what he was doing back home in terms of continuing his profession and offering his expertise. He responded negatively, stating that he found it extremely challenging to compete with the faster, younger, and 'savvier' fellow Indians.

Well, Sagar did change his mind about that. Before we fly back home, he whispered to me something that sounded totally opposite to what he'd said previously. "You know, Mohamed," he said in a blissful tone as we climbed down the stairs of Unity Hospital a day after my dad's surgery, "if I could be of help to my dear friend Ali, maybe I could help many others who need similar assistance. You see, I can be someone whom patients can rely on to find specific guidance on the best available medical care and doctors. I'm sure those young Indians can't outperform me on this one—no way!"

Viewing the situation from this fresh angle, Sagar realized that there would be little or no replacement for his particular expertise for those who needed it most. He discovered that he could be the one and only medical tour guide for a specific category of clients. He had a broad understanding of the medical landscape across Mangalore and Bangalore, the two cities he often moved between. Additionally, his background knowledge and interest in certain medical issues for specific patients were solid. All of this made him a unique go-to person for finding solutions that would otherwise be more difficult, slow, or insufficient. Furthermore, Sagar knew multiple Indian languages, as well as English and Arabic, and he was keenly acquainted with Arabic culture thanks to his extensive work experience in the Middle East.

Sagar was 'The One' due to several attributes he possessed, not just one. If he had relied on only one aspect—say, knowing the geographical details of the medical services and doctors available—he would have fallen into a category crowded with many others. It was the sum of everything he was and knew that gave him the confidence to progress and offer his help in a way that others couldn't, no matter how fast or savvy they appeared.

Moreover, it took Sagar a 'case'—my dad's—to realize this valuable insight. He was drawn into a scenario that demanded his critical and timely intervention, leading to a happy ending and one of his life's most significant contributions. Sagar possessed these abilities even before he received our email or learned anything about dad. Yet, according to our initial conversation, he was unaware of the gifts that only he and no one else could provide, to give new life to a man he had shared a significant part of his life with.

Even Sagar's unique abilities remained a mystery to him until someone needed them. When the time was right, Sagar's understanding of who he was, what he could do, and—most importantly—how he could help others, underwent a significant shift. This was just one aspect of Sagar's 'One and Only' service to the benefit of others. What if Sagar were placed in different situations that required his other talents and strengths to intervene? Just as his unique 'medical guide' skills emerged to solve one type of problem, another set of Sagar's abilities could surface to address challenges at a different level for another kind of case.

What makes us unique in our contributions is a cluster of strengths that come together to resolve complicated situations. However, it is the emergence of these situations that brings out the unique set of skills we possess but may be unaware of and have acted indifferently toward.

> What makes us unique in our contributions is a cluster of strengths that come together to resolve complicated situations.

My 'One and Only' Dad

My dad was 'The One And Only' too. His passion as an air fueling operations expert accompanied us at every junction in our trip. In fact, I don't recall travelling with dad in the years before this particular trip when he wasted an opportunity to talk about the types of aircrafts we viewed through the airport's wide glass shields. Let alone giving a more detailed explanation of the airplane we were about to board.

Sometimes, he would just sit next to the boarding gate, staring at the fueling vehicles passing to and from the parked aircraft. His gaze at the machines, operators, and vehicles moving in all directions was one of joy and nostalgia. He was like the beekeeper who understands and relishes the interconnectedness of what otherwise, would be nothing more than a chaotic scene that stresses me—the safety practitioner—wondering and wishing that no one gets hurt on this messy airport ramp.

But another event brought a special smile to my dad's heart and life years earlier. My father retired from his job sometime in the '90s. However, years after his retirement, he was approached by one of the newly built airports in the region. Out of many air fueling experts, he was the preferred option, not only because of his extensive experience but also due to a combination of strengths—not just one aspect alone. His mix of long experience, deep knowledge, exceptional grasp of global air fueling standards, and strong communication skills was the reason he, and no one else, was chosen to train the aircraft fueling crew at that airport.

I can still remember how that six-month contract had brought much happiness to him at the time. Like Sagar, my father, years after his retirement, was still being sought after by clients who appreciated his unique contributions to meeting their needs. The interesting part is that I witnessed the same pattern in my case as well as in Sagar's. What made my dad 'The One And Only' choice for the airport company were mainly two reasons. First, he possessed a number of strengths (not just one) that the client aimed to find in one person. Second, dad didn't know he was 'The One And Only' until he came across someone, an entity, who needed his unique combination of skills. Before that, he probably saw himself as a professional who was no longer needed by his company and thought that he could easily be replaced.

There's a third part. When we bring together all three of us—Sagar, my father, and me—we find that we have something in common.

We were all retired at the time we discovered our 'One And Only' (OAO) contributions. Well, Sagar and dad were officially retired, while I had resigned. Nevertheless, we were all at a stage where people in our position might consider it too late to be of any significance in our industry or profession. On the contrary, our experiences showed that the opposite was true. Progress in our careers and life, in general, allowed us to 'accumulate' experiences that worked in our favor. Many ingredients were added throughout our vocational lives, resulting in a dish that was almost impossible to replicate.

The more you advance in life, the more experiences you collect along the way. The longer you travel, the more memories and artifacts you add to your 'treasure box'. This accumulation—whether willingly or not—makes you one of the 'fewer' available experts.

Do you understand my point? This paradox works for you, not against you. You are 'The One And Only' because of the 'many' you have and are. The more, the merrier. The messier the merrier.

2013

What a year! From April to June! From Manama to Mumbai to Mangalore to Saudi Arabia! These events seemed disconnected, gathered only on the 2013 calendar. Yet, nothing can be as connected as these dots. To witness three people going through similar transformational journeys in one single year was anything but a coincidence.

Dad's dream, his desire to see Sagar and eventually be cured of a disease we hadn't known.

Sagar's doubt and then certainty about his ability to give more than he thought he could, better than anyone else.

And I declined all the Saudi clients' requests to join the project until I discovered I was their one and only choice.

In less than six months, I had to go through strenuous situations that were circumstantially different but essentially similar. They all had one message for me: You are 'The One And Only'. Not only me, but also dad and Sagar. In other words, I am not the only 'One And Only'; everyone is.

> I am not the only 'One And Only'; everyone is.

I didn't think the events of 2013 would travel with me for the rest of my life. But year after year, I saw how these events, their effects, and the messages they carried slowly became a growing part of the fabric of my professional life—and, subsequently, my whole life. My attention has zoomed in more on the unique blend of characteristics I have possessed over time. I started observing how clustering different pieces of experiences created inimitable sets of DNA[7] that quickly appealed to specific markets, clients, and demands. This new appreciative view of who I am and what I can offer encouraged me to stick to—well, who I am.

If my complex combination of pieces made me an ideal option for a client, then I might as well follow this pattern. Rather than be repulsed by my diverse strengths, I began to see how they empowered me in excellent ways. I started studying why certain programs I delivered and products I created appealed highly to certain clients and target audiences. I learned how the fusion of several features in a particular training program, for instance, was the prime reason for their unmatched success.

Now, my products have 'The One And Only' quality. So, I walked faster toward that path, not away from it.

I never looked back again.

> So, I walked faster toward that path, not away from it.
>
> I never looked back again.

***

---

[7] DNA Here the DNA is being used as a metaphor.

"The 'One And Only' program prompted me to revisit my past experiences and talents, leading to the creation of new business opportunities. Inspired by the program, I soon launched a new company based on this concept. Two years later, the 'One And Only' philosophy continues to guide the expansion and growth of my business."

– Mazen Al-Sadat
Head of Corporate Innovation,
Entrepreneur, Saudi Arabia

*** *** ***

Take A Moment And Think:

- In addition to your past expertise and skills, what other gains have you made? Consider the people you met, the connections you built, and the friends you made. Can they be added to your current strengths?
- What contributions did you make in the past to your workplace, coworkers, customers, community, industry, and professional network?
- Have the services you've generously provided gone in vain, or will they return to serve YOU in new and unexpected ways?
- Can you picture how your strengths from your best and easiest times in the past could be most helpful to you in your most challenging circumstances now?
- Can we agree on a modified definition of a miracle at work: when seemingly unconnected aspects of your professional past, present, and future come together to birth a brand-new child that was intended to revitalize your life and extend your legacy?

Your thoughts here:

*** *** ***

CHAPTER 10

THE 'OAO' FACTOR

*T*he events of 2013 have only awakened me to this truth, which I will confidently call the 'OAO Factor'. I won't be able to invest in this discovery if I don't turn it from a singled-out fact to a universal factor, i.e. the 'OAO Factor'.

If I ended the journey at the juncture where the Saudi project concluded, or where my father was miraculously cured, I would enjoy nothing beyond the anecdotal aspect of a memory told and treasured. To invest in the treasures of that expedition, the OAO fact had to become a 'factor' penetrating every aspect of my life, particularly in the area where it applied most powerfully: my career.

Slowly, I began to witness and experience the unique benefits and fruits of applying the 'OAO Factor'. The more benefits I received, the bolder I became in adopting the 'OAO Factor' in my subsequent endeavors—as a rule, not as an exception.

Yes, it's true that I am 'The One And Only'. You Are 'The One And Only'. Every single human on this planet is 'The One and Only'. But to enjoy this universal truth, we need to take it from concept to practice, and from a lesson learned to an applicable law: the 'One and Only Factor,' which I shall hereafter refer to as the 'OAO Factor'.

Let me walk you through SEVEN major takeaways on putting the 'OAO Factor' to work. These takeaways have directly benefited my career life and success following 2013.

Moreover, many of those who came across the 'OAO Factor' during my OAO speaking and training programs over the past ten years have reported back to me on how they were also able to turn their careers around. Likewise, I hope they will impact yours.

1. Waste:

Steve Jobs' famous quote says it best: "You can't connect the dots looking forward; you can only connect them looking backward. So, you have to trust that the dots will somehow connect in your future."

The incongruence between all my previous decisions, paths, and choices seemed nothing more than random chaos, making me look like a visionless, disorganized individual living by the virtue of accident. I kept moving through life, open to better possibilities, hoping that the next phase would erase the sins of my previous inconsistent and erroneous choices.

With every setback I experienced, I placed the blame solely on myself: my lack of goal setting, my ever-distracted mind, and my inability to live a purposeful life. I attributed every missed opportunity, every lost financial gain, and every career success I didn't achieve to my muddled self and my messy way of living. Yet, I had no choice but to move forward, picking anything and everything that would help me survive in an increasingly complex job market that kept refining and redefining what career success meant. This had led me to collecting more and more pieces, causing the old and new ones to pile up and make things seem even more disconnected and cluttered.

Go back to all your experiences, because none of them was a waste.

And then, everything connected. It took me almost a whole year, walking through an unknown, dark tunnel, to emerge at the other end with a new light. The events of 2013 made sense of everything that didn't make sense before. No, I did not connect the dots myself. The rigorous events, culminating in the phone call with the Saudi client, caused all the scattered dots to fly from the far corners of my life and connect in harmony.

Yes, I came to realize that my life events weren't accidental, but rather interconnected through one seemingly chance occurrence. But it didn't have to stay that way. Once I grasped the idea, I made a deliberate attempt to turn the 'connecting-the-dots' of my life from accidental to intentional. How? More on this in the remaining points.

> I made a deliberate attempt to turn the 'connecting-the-dots' of my life from accidental to intentional.

2. Adding Is Subtracting

Growing up is—by definition—days, months, and years added to your life. Yes, and also experiences. My career had the lion's share of 'adding'. I accumulated accolades, achievements, certifications, designations, titles, credentials—the list is long.

And like many others, I did all this to stand out; that is, to become one of the few. I believed that by adding more credentials—bigger titles, higher qualifications, and more widely recognized certifications—I would gain significance and stand out from competition. This way, I would be shortlisted and rise to the top of the list, a place harder and costlier for others to reach.

Dig deep to reach your precious diamonds, and don't be pulled in by the sandcastles that others are happy with.

In my industry, occupational health and safety, for example, I felt the need to go through a sequence of professional development programs offered by different organizations. I wanted to be recognized not just as a credible expert in my field, but as one of its leading authorities.

I could choose from an array of academic institutions, professional bodies, global organizations, and international federations, each of them offering an exhaustive list of programs that lead to glittering titles. Yum yum! Let me have a 'diploma' from this institute, a 'membership' from that association, and a dash of 'accreditation' from this esteemed organization. More, more, and more—to be listed among the rare, the few, and the significant.

Bottom line: to stand out, I had to add more. Plurality is the path to singularity.

However, it wasn't until 2013 that I realized the ugly side of adding more in this manner. Apart from enriching the pockets of academic and professional institutions (don't get me wrong; these organizations do a good job of 'adding more' to your professional development), I found myself facing increased confusion about how I perceived my career dashboard. The worst part was that with each accolade I added—in an effort to distance myself from the competition in my circle—I inadvertently entered another crowded circle.

> Plurality is the path to singularity.

Tricky, isn't it? You aimed to escape the crowded space of your industry by venturing into new territory, only to find yourself lost in yet another crowd.

The 2013 experience, however, offered me a new perspective on what really makes you stand out in your industry. Admittedly, it still involves adding. It goes something like this: to stand out and be among the few, you do need to add more credentials. But the credentials you add in this case are not external credentials that make you common with many other individuals (and ultimately win a race, only to enter another). I am talking about those little INNER pieces you can patch together to create a unique and unparalleled blend. Unlike the outer credentials, which are potentially (and actually) accessible to anyone else and require long and laborious pursuits, your inner credentials are available within you—right away—right away–and they are accessible only to you and no one else.

> Your inner credentials are available within you—right away—and they are accessible only to you and no one else.

Once again, plurality is the path to singularity. What the 'OAO Factor' taught me was that a faster route to being singled out is adding layers of credentials to form a matchless mosaic of expertise. More accurately, imagine an inverted pyramid: the deeper you go, the narrower it becomes. By ADDING more layers downward, you are actually subtracting from the pyramid's mass until you reach the bottom, where the peak rests. Paradoxically, the top lies at the bottom. To reach that point, I had to go—unknowingly—through an elimination process by adding more features that the client wanted in me all at once. The client kept providing more reasons why I was the single preferred option for their mission. By ADDING more reasons for choosing me over others (such as electrical engineering, power generation, 'SMS' safety accreditation, and public speaking), he was, in essence, ruling out (or subtracting) all other options.

Adding is subtracting.

3. The Messier, the Merrier

Have you watched the movie 'The Imitation Game'? I have, more times than I can remember. The movie is full of thought-provoking messages and lessons. One that struck me the most has a subtle yet strong link to the 'One And Only Factor'. The one and only Alan Turing (played by Benedict Cumberbatch), a brilliant mathematician and computer scientist—dubbed 'the father of computer science' —leads a team of codebreakers to decipher the codes of Enigma, a machine used by the Germans during World War II in almost every radio communication. To achieve this, the team—led by Turing—developed a machine called 'Bombe'. If you have watched the movie, you know what the 'Bombe' machine looked like: a huge wall of complicated rotating parts that operated to match the rotating wheels in the German Enigma machine. In other words, the British Bombe machine was 'imitating' the Enigma mechanism so that it could understand the content of the messages sent by the Germans, intercepted by British intelligence, but otherwise could not be cracked.

Funny as it may sound, and as much as I love the movie and its plot, the point I'm eager to make is this: it took a brilliant team of scientists, substantial funding, and a long time to crack the codes of Enigma (not to mention the losses the British had to endure before achieving that goal). Why? Because it was too 'complicated'. What does that have to do with my 2013 experience? Everything.

Remember my messy CV? It turned out that the messiness I grumbled about was a blessing in disguise. The 'bundle' of features my client wanted and found in me was the reason his options were reduced to ONE. I became a complicated combination of qualities that was so unique it was almost impossible to find in anyone else at the time. It was as if the client had published a special vacancy ad, and the conditions listed could only be met by a single candidate, resulting in just ONE applicant. And that was me.

The messier, the merrier: your complex blend is what makes you impossible to imitate.

The 'OAO Factor' states that each of us is naturally 'encrypted'. The seemingly clashing set of skills creates endless possibilities for unique services or products we can offer our clients, while remaining immune to imitation at the same time. Each of these products and services come from within us, from our lives and the myriad of experiences. The more components each product or service contains, the more difficult it is to copy or imitate.

We live in a world of ruthless competition and unapologetic counterfeiting. Education and training—my core practice—are no exception. In almost any field or industry, trainers and experts offer solutions that can easily be (and often are) imitated. When we value the complexity of our messy expertise, we are affirming our uniqueness and saying yes to being imitation-proof.

> When we value the complexity of our messy expertise, we are affirming our uniqueness and saying yes to being imitation-proof.

This became increasingly evident to me after 2013. Like the unique combination my Saudi client made me see, I began to see other cases where different combinations of my skills were required.

I designed dozens of programs and products from mixtures of my natural abilities, and this made my programs—in essence—inimitable.

Is your career messy? Relax; it means your career and what you have to offer are essentially immune to imitation. But you have to do the work. Be conscious of how your many skills can, together, form a unique solution to address a specific pain in your world. The best part is that you won't have to endure the pain and panic of counterfeit threats.

After all, the more the merrier. The messier, the merrier.

4. A Jack Of All Trades?

'A jack of all trades is a master of none!' You've heard this before, right?

Often used in a negative context, it criticizes someone (or yourself) for being skilled and experienced in various fields, suggesting that you are not a master of any one in particular.

This made total sense to many people for many, many years. I used to believe in it until 2013. The Saudi client was looking for a number of 'trades', all of which I possessed. Admittedly, he didn't insist on or inquire about my mastery in all of them. It was enough for him that I had a 'practical background' in each and a mastery level in at least two. I became his 'One And Only' because of my diverse trades—not just one.

This is not a debate on 'generalist vs. specialist' (although it does trigger it). I encourage you to explore the recent research and discussions on a topic that is affecting our careers—and how we perceive them—in unprecedented ways. In our rapidly changing world, it goes without saying that almost none of us—professionals—has evaded, or will evade, the dilemma of whether to specialize in a certain area or remain broadly qualified in all that we know and do.

The 'OAO Factor' provided me with the answer: you don't have to choose between the two. By definition, a dilemma is a situation in which a difficult choice must be made between two or more alternatives. The 'OAO Factor' asks: are you really in that situation? It's difficult only if you feel you have to choose, but the truth is, you have already made a choice. You already have a career built on many choices, changes and competencies.

The 'OAO Factor' relieves you of the pain of choosing between 'generalist' and 'specialist'. The only choice you will need to make will provide you with the benefits of BOTH: 'generalist' and 'specialist'. Yes, you read that right. Here's how it works:

1. You go back to all your previous pieces and dots (the choices that made you the messy expert you are today).
2. Consciously select a number of those pieces.
3. Put them together in a bundle that forms a practical solution for a need or problem out there.
4. Introduce yourself as a 'specialist' who can tackle this issue with a unique solution (which you and I both know you developed through the 'generalist' approach you applied in point 3).

By adopting this, you are NOT in a difficult situation where you must choose between the benefits of being a 'generalist' or a 'specialist'. You are combining the advantages of both, by being both a generalist and a specialist.

What you have just done is solve a specific problem by leveraging several areas of your expertise as a GENERALIST while presenting yourself as a unique expert in addressing this problem as a SPECIALIST.

This way, you no longer have to ask: "Should I be a generalist or a specialist?"

Because you are neither. You are both.

You are a 'gespecialist'.

> This way, you no longer have to ask: "Should I be a generalist or a specialist?"
>
> Because you are neither. You are both.
>
> You are a 'gespecialist'!

Be a 'Gespecialist': bring the ingredients together and invent a new dish.

With this new term—and reality—I may claim to have provided a new angle to the ongoing 'generalist vs. specialist' debate. The answer that the 'OAO Factor' offers is not to reject one in favor of the other, but to reconcile both.

I now wonder if the person who originated the 'jack of all trades' quote (and the unending quarrel) would agree with me. Even better, I hope he would approve of the idea of a 'gespecialist' as at least a good application of his original—and complete—quote:

'A jack of all trades is a master of none, but oftentimes better than a master of one!' — 'The One And Only' William Shakespeare.

5. To Chase Or Be Chased?

'Headhunted!' Most of us professionals enjoy the fact (or fantasy) of being headhunted for a job, rather than simply being accepted for it. If we are asked what we do, we typically respond with, 'I am working as a [position] for [company]', without mentioning how we got there—unless we were headhunted. In that case, we make sure to stress that part.

Regardless of the job we were headhunted for, its rank, the package offered, or whether we actually ended up accepting the offer, the sheer fact that 'I was chosen for this mission' brings a whole range of sentiments to the forefront of how we perceive ourselves and our expertise.

"I am sought-after."

"The market recognizes my unique ability and contribution."

"They saw in me what I couldn't see in myself."

"I am of special value to this or that industry."

"I am capable of doing – and earning – more than what I thought I could."

Do I need to remind you that in 2013, I didn't chase after the opportunity with the Saudi company—I was chosen and pursued? No, I don't. But I do need to tell you that since that 'accident', I became aware that, in the future, I don't have to wait for random 'accidents'.

I started thinking: if this client chased me for a particular reason, which I hadn't paid attention to (the 'OAO Factor'), what if I start paying more attention to the reasons that attract higher-quality clients and projects? In plain words, I began luring the market I want to work in by becoming the OAO (One and Only) option it has, or the OAO target it wants to hunt.

Rather than waiting for clients to randomly discover reasons to hire me or partner with me, I consciously create those reasons for them to do so. This way, those reasons become the rule, not a random occurrence. It may look like the market is hunting and chasing me, but in fact, I am the one who has lured them into the spot where I hunt them.

And before you judge me, let me say I didn't achieve this by pretending to be someone I'm not. Nor did I stack up deceptive baits of fancy titles and expertise. Doing all that just to convince the other party that I was worthy of their sole and biggest investment would be faking and fabricating, not factual. The 'OAO Factor' teaches the exact opposite. By presenting the truth of who you are—the whole truth, and nothing but the truth—the market will swiftly identify you as the OAO solution it's looking for. And thus, it will chase you down, rather than the other way around.

To chase or to be chased?

If there's anything that makes me want to watch the movie Kung Fu Panda again and again (besides the fact that it's a masterpiece by all measures), it's what Po, the main character (a panda), discovers by accident. Po initially believes that what makes a true Kung Fu warrior is physical strength and combat skills. However, as his journey progresses, he realizes that inner strength is the key that unlocks his potential as the OAO Dragon Warrior.

Po is a big fan of the Furious Five, the warriors trained and nurtured in the Jade Palace by Master Shifu. He copies their styles in his room above the restaurant kitchen where he works as a waiter. Even after he is 'chosen' by Master Oogway as the Dragon Warrior, he continues to work hard to measure up to his colleagues' levels in all combat arts and skills.

When Po is given the Dragon Scroll, which is supposed to turn him into the Dragon Warrior, he discovers it is a blank metallic page that does nothing but reflect his own face. So, while the OAO chased and chosen Dragon Warrior is Po, it is only when he realizes—and uses—who he truly is and his true inner strength that he truly becomes the Dragon Warrior.

Stop hiding behind your unrealistically customized and incomplete CV. Open your Dragon Scroll and look carefully—who do you see? That ONE you're looking at is the OAO who will be chosen and chased.

6. The Big Picture

"So you got lucky," said one of the participants following a recent 'One And Only' keynote I delivered. "The Saudi company contacted you because they knew you would fulfill a need they had."

Exactly! A need. A gap. A problem. Every entity, every organization, and every market has them, and they will always have them as long as they exist and seek to evolve and develop. It's part of the improvement cycle. The question is: which problem will you be a solution for? Which need will you fulfill? Which organization can you help?

> The question is: which problem will you be a solution for? Which need will you fulfill? Which organization can you help?

Yes, I was lucky to get the call. But the connection of the dots wasn't a coincidence. It follows a pattern, and if you understand that pattern, you can make it happen and repeat it. If the pattern is a natural phenomenon in the wheel of life, then you can actually predict these 'lucky' moments. What is luck, anyway? The Roman philosopher Seneca described it as, "luck is what happens when preparation meets opportunity."

Imagine organizations as large jigsaw puzzles with some missing pieces. These pieces represent what we, in business terms, call 'gaps'. These gaps signify needs that the organization must address to continue surviving and thriving. They are, therefore, in constant search of solutions to fill these gaps, both internally and externally. In other words, they're looking for something or someone that can complete what they see as 'the missing piece'. Until they find that piece, the gap remains unfilled, and the big picture—the organization's jigsaw puzzle—remains incomplete and unsolved.

You see it as an 'opportunity'. After all, isn't that what we call a job vacancy, whether internally or externally? That 'opening' is for you to consider and decide if you are the answer.

Your completed puzzle will solve a bigger puzzle.

The 'OAO Factor' is a reverse-engineering of the 'luck factor'. The way that gentleman described my incident with the Saudi client was in the context of luck: "You were in a mess. The Saudi client saw in your mess a solution for their mess – or need. They called you, and you got the job."

The 'OAO Factor', on the other hand, suggests that you should open your eyes to opportunities, look around in your organization and other organizations for missing pieces. See which gaps you can fill, pick up your pieces, and arrange them so that they serve that gap or need. Offer yourself as the 'missing piece' in the big jigsaw puzzle.

More often than not, once you collect and complete your pieces, connect the dots of your career, and solve your puzzle, you won't have to wait long before you receive the next 'lucky' call. Why? Because only when you do so, you become so unique that you *cannot* be ignored or unnoticed.

Pick up your scattered pieces. Solve your puzzle. Become a unique piece that a bigger puzzle is looking for. Get in there and complete that puzzle like any irreplaceable piece in a jigsaw. You will then understand not only that you are a part of the bigger universal puzzle, but also how you fit within it. And when that happens, you will never again see yourself as a redundant or random piece in the world. You will enjoy the realization that you are never just a number but the One And Only.

7. Peace

Peace of mind. Peace of heart. Peace of life. There's no one who doesn't yearn for inner, lasting peace. In fact, our restless hustle in life is a subtle determination to get a piece of that peace before we 'rest in peace'.

> Our restless hustle in life is a subtle determination to get a piece of that peace before we 'rest in peace'.

For most of our lives—actually, for the strongest and most vital part of it—we will be consumed by our work, whether in the form of jobs or businesses. However, as we take our first steps in our career lives, we begin to notice that this path is anything but peaceful. We recognize how ferocious it is to carve our way to 'success'. Conventional wisdom suggests— and indeed recognizes—that a career is akin to struggle, hustle, and fighting. There can be no successful career without a mix of blood, sweat, and tears. Right?

Not really, says the 'OAO Factor'.

Anyone who has lived a career of any length or intensity (and who hasn't?!) will recognize these THREE phenomena as unavoidable, inescapable, and inevitable:

1. Competition.
2. Comparison.
3. Copying.

Each one poses a perceived threat that unveils itself in different forms and phases of our careers. They appear only to impede or interfere with our progress. A new product competing with ours, a coworker whom my superiors started comparing me with, and a company that has managed to copy my signature product. The worst part is that these 'threats' convince us to deal with them—or else we're done for.

These side battles that we didn't plan for, will only delay and divert us from our career's main progress. Moreover, we risk being slowly poisoned by their subtle effects. My insecurity grows as other professionals attract more opportunities than I do. My self-esteem declines when a younger startup gains more ground and profits than I do. My anxiety spikes as I witness rivals introducing services or solutions faster and better than mine.

Insecurity. Self-doubt. Anxiety. Envy. Fear. These cannot coexist with peace. Guess which one is forced to withdraw? Peace, of course. Primarily because we are programmed to believe that competition, comparison, and copy are inevitable parts of anyone's career, and thus, we accept them as normal. When we do so, we accept the venom they bring to our minds, bodies, and lives.

But I am here to tell you that you don't have to accept all this to be successful in your career. I know what you're thinking, and before you ask, I'll address it:

How can you offer the 'One And Only' factor and concept as 'the' solution for the three stealers of peace (competition, comparison, and copy)? The OAO idea is the culprit, the cause, not the cure. Anyone who wants to be the OAO must experience these three Cs. In fact, if you want to reach that sweet, matchless spot where 'no one's like me', the threat of competition, comparison, and copying becomes even fiercer. So, by definition, the 'OAO Factor' is the cause, not the antidote, to the peace-stripping venom.

This is a fair and expected argument. Let me address it with both a short answer and a longer one.

The short answer is: the above applies to those who seek to 'become' the OAO, not realizing that they already 'are' the OAO. The former is linked to a negative perspective, which believes—like the majority around them—that one must observe and overpower others to triumph. The latter belongs to a positive perspective, which recognizes that "I am ALREADY the OAO," and thus there's no need to fear others' competition, comparison, and copying. They become irrelevant by default.

Okay, that wasn't too short. But it is, compared to the longer answer that's coming. Let me break down each threat—starting with the most obvious one, Copy—and explain how the 'OAO Factor' addresses each in a logical and organic way:

1. Copy

Have you ever worried that someone might copy your fingerprints to gain access to your property and take what's yours? No, for the simple reason that it's almost impossible to do so. Okay, maybe it is possible, given the advanced level technology has reached. But do I really need to calculate the costs one would incur to create a profile of your fingerprints, let alone make a duplicate and use it?!

Likewise, anyone's greed and ill intentions will fall short when it comes to trying to copy your 'OAO' experience and the skills you've poured into a messy product or service. "It's just not worth it," I imagine them saying, even before attempting any action.

This is the kind of peace that the 'OAO Factor' enables you to experience. You, along with your mosaic of talents and expertise, make a masterpiece that is too difficult to counterfeit. As professionals, we need to better the world we're serving through original ideas and meaningful innovation. Yet, the mere fear of being copied is capable of stripping away our confidence and composure.

"We have no time to lose."

"Let's finish this and present it to the market before someone else does."

"Let me launch the product with all its flaws before someone else figures it out."

The urgency in these statements reflects a race to win rather than a race to save and serve humanity. Undoubtedly, this rush compromises process excellence, quality, and meticulousness. It also robs its creators of serenity, psychological safety, and even sanity, all for the sake of getting—and staying—ahead of the competition (which we will address next).

Those who believe in and apply the 'OAO Factor' are also in the midst of this crazy rush and race. Yet, they are immune to the fears and threats of 'copy' and 'counterfeit'. They understand that the good they create for the world is as complex and non-replicable as their fingerprints.

2. Competition

Like copy, competition troubles us professionals and prevents us from being still or at peace. The difference, however, is that we treat copy as ill and evil, whereas we view competition as healthy. At least the type we allow ourselves to engage in must be 'healthy', right? I'm not going to debate that. Competition is good and healthy as long as it positively serves all parties involved: the competitors, the market, and the people who benefit from this competition—primarily the customers.

But I assume you agree with me that even in healthy competitions, the elements of fear, insecurity and rush do persist. You don't need much memory power to recall a time when a colleague's performance threatened your chances of getting the promotion you both vied for. Or the rush of blood to your head when you read that headline about a product that outperforms and underprices your company's offering. Whether the competition is healthy or not, its impact on your peace of mind and inner security is definitely NOT healthy.

You justify the means—frequent inner turbulence and a constant fear of falling behind—as long as they lead you to the end: the worthwhile destination of staying ahead.

Going back to the fingerprint metaphor, do you really fear that someone might have a fingerprint profile that's better than yours? No, you absolutely do not care. That's because you are certain that your fingerprint gives you access to places and opportunities that your competition cannot reach. Not only do you NOT worry, you are actually a winner–with no one else being a loser.

This is where the 'OAO Factor' aims to take you—a place where 'competition is irrelevant', as the 'Blue Ocean' strategy puts it. Like your 'One and Only' fingerprint profile, you wake up to the undisputed truth that your career also has a complex 'One and Only' profile. Only by embracing this uniqueness can you touch and transform your world in an undisputed, magical, and magnificent way.

> Only by embracing this uniqueness can you touch and transform your world in an undisputed, magical, and magnificent way.

Kevin Kelly, the founding executive editor of Wired magazine and a former editor and publisher of Whole Earth Review, reportedly said: "Don't be the best. Be the only." In a short clip from a longer interview, he explains what he means by this: "You want to be doing something where it's hard to explain to your mother what it is that you do."

This captures the essence of what the 'OAO Factor' teaches. Instead of wasting your energy on becoming the best, the fastest, the brightest, or the most famous—all of which are peace-killing weapons—focus your efforts on being the best version of who you are and what you do. By doing so, you achieve both: standing out from the competition (a gentler way to stay ahead of rivals) and maintaining your inner peace without getting caught up in unending, ferocious rivalries.

> Instead of wasting your energy on becoming the best, the fastest, the brightest, or the most famous—all of which are peace-killing weapons—focus your efforts on being the best version of who you are and what you do.

3. Comparison

"They have something I don't have." This is how we fall prey to comparison on a daily basis. Our unmindful daily struggle is to 'keep up with the Joneses' in almost everything: how much we earn, where and how we live, what we drive, how we look, and even how we raise our children.

Our careers and jobs are not safe from the deadly venom of comparison. In fact, comparing our careers—down to the tiniest details—with those of others consumes a significant portion of our lives. The way we see ourselves, through the lens of what we do for a living, makes life even more difficult. Yet, the funny thing about comparison is that it is, by definition, self-destructive. Like venom, comparison carries its antidote within it.

> Like venom, comparison carries its antidote within it.

Think of your fingerprints again. Who on earth wishes they had fingerprints identical to someone else's?! We are comfortable, at peace, and even happy knowing our fingerprints have no match in the entire world. We never look at someone else's fingerprints as better or prettier than ours. Our fingerprints, and everyone else's, are simply fingerprints. And we're all happy with them as they are. It's not like we lack or have lost something.

With this, a revised definition of 'comparison' is: "They have something I don't, and I have something they don't." And that's totally okay.

See! It's no longer an issue. The 'OAO Factor' did it again!

When you learn and live as 'The One and Only', there is no room for feelings of inferiority or superiority. There is no 'better than' or 'worse than'. There are only us humans, who have one thing in common: we are different. None of us is, has been, or ever will be identical to anyone else.

If true joy is your aim, which it is, then you'll find it in being different from others—and in knowing that they are unable to be like you, just as you are unable to be like them. This is a reason for celebration, not separation. You celebrate your uniqueness, but you also celebrate everyone else's uniqueness and how, together, we make a unique fabric called humanity.

This, my dear readers, is called true PEACE.

Your uniqueness brings peace to you. Your peace will impact world peace.

> When you learn and live as 'The One and Only', there is no room for feelings of inferiority or superiority.

A Final Word About Peace

As I see it, the 3 Cs (copy, competition, and comparison) represent the inevitable axis of anxiety and unrest for every professional in almost every career. Countless avenues intersect and radiate from this axis. Imagine the extraordinary measures people take to sidestep the perils of the 3 Cs: fraud, fabrication, faking, lying, misinformation, abuse of power, false accusations, defamation, plagiarism, piracy, infringement, corruption—you name it. This is not to mention the internal damage and disturbance one would incur in the form of envy, depression, discontent, misery, loss of self-esteem, hate, grudge, resentment—you name it.

And if your career takes up most of your life—which it does—then the most vital and valuable portion of your life is afflicted by the 3Cs.

The good news is: it doesn't have to be that way. The 'OAO Factor' asserts that just because the 3 Cs are real and inescapable in every professional's path, it doesn't mean we have to fall easy prey to them. No sensible person would intentionally and consciously sabotage their physical, mental, and psychological well-being for the sake of financial success. In my book—and in any book—that's failure, not success.

Yet, in the meantime, the 'OAO Factor' also acknowledges that we are human. And being exposed to the dark side of these peace-killing practices and threats is natural—whether we engage in them as volunteers or as victims. However, the solution is not to act indifferently to these threats, nor adopt a mentality of renunciation and leave everything behind. Denial is defeat. Defiance, on the other hand, is victory.

When you discover that you are 'The One And Only', everything falls into place. Attempting to thoroughly and expansively treat every single threat from competition, copying or comparison is just a waste of time and life. And to believe that you have no choice but to eternally engage in these 'wars' cannot be farther from the truth. Not to mention that this engagement is the best recipe to get distracted and deviate from your main career track and progress.

Once you believe in, behold, and embrace being 'The One And Only', you defuse and defeat all these threats without having to face and fix them one by one. It's a one big 'POWER' button you press and all your defenses and guards against peace-trolls are activated.

Stay true to yourself, to your 'One And Only' self, and live it as deeply and widely as you can. You will begin to witness the inner joy of being who you truly are, happy with all the 'mess' you have, knowing that you encompass a summation that is impossible to compare, copy, or compete with.

> You celebrate your uniqueness, but you also celebrate everyone else's uniqueness and how, together, we make a unique fabric called humanity.

***

"My corporate journey was Horizontal with lots of learnings across various products and involved different Physics. I felt an identity crisis in spite of contributing more, most of the work was niche in medical devices. And it doesn't fit into any of the conventional roles in our domain or industry. After attending the program in Colombo, I changed my LinkedIn Profile headline as 'The OAO Multiphysics Simulations leader in #Med in #India..' Everyone looked at this as a gesture of arrogance. But actually I feel this headline as being spiritual. Having pride in the journey that life has offered me, with gratitude. I had an unique opportunity to work on a wide variety of advanced engineering activities and couldn't find it meaningful though it's my passion. But today, my UVP[8] is 'Holistic approach to Product design'. I wished

---

[8]UVP: Unique Value Proposition

for a conventional career path but that wouldn't have helped me stand out in a crowded marketplace as an entrepreneur. We can only grow through what we go through. Embracing all our unique views, ideas, experiences, education, successes, failures, thoughts, feelings, knowledge, skills, talents is important. A combination of any of these is a niche and OAO. We can only find the hidden treasure later, after the dots get connected. The story of every journey is OAO!"

– Rajesh "Multiphysics"
Entrepreneur, India

CHAPTER 11

YOU ARE THE ONE AND ONLY

*Y*ou are the One And Only, you always have been, and you will always be. It's the rational, logical, and pure reality.

But it's a reality that's better lived than put to rest.

A Road Map?

Hmm! Not exactly. I was clear with myself, right from the start of writing this book, that I didn't want it to be a strict how-to manual. That would go against the very spirit of the book: to be innovative and build *your* own plan and pathway from the unique mix these pages inspired you to create.

In 'The One And Only' speaking program, I made it a habit to avoid showering the attendees with typical 'Do's and Don'ts' lists. The results astonished me as many attendees reported taking life-changing steps and leaps: starting a new business, shifting careers, reverting to previous passions, revitalizing a sleeping dream, staying where they are but with greater content and peace, writing a book, starting a project, speeding up their promotions, and the list goes on.

Likewise, I hope every reader of this book will receive it in their own way, have different takeaways, and translate it into unique and specific actions they will adopt in their lives.

Each will 'Unleash A New Niche'.

That's the whole point of the book. So why undermine its novelty and brilliance by adding a bunch of boundaries called 'action plan' or 'road map' or whatever?

That said, I'm also aware that if you've reached this point in the book, you're probably more ready than ever to take ACTION. Having been blessed with thousands of people who showed undeniable eagerness to take positive steps in their lives following 'The One And Only' speaking program, it would be indifferent of me to stop here and 'call it a day' without answering your inner, deepest call.

So, allow me to help you with these FIVE points (notice I didn't call them steps or actions). Take them as you wish. But they are my 'way forward' gift to you—a practical transition from the book to your real life.

1) Believe

"You Are The One And Only." Notice I didn't say "You will be…" or "You can become…" the one and only. Being the one and only is not a potential or possibility. It's a reality. And if something is a reality but left unbelieved, then that reality serves no one—especially the one who disbelieves it.

The point, the central point, is to believe. When you start to believe, even in the tiniest and most blurred ways, that you are 'The One And Only', behold this belief. Foster it. Nurture it. Make a habit of applying this belief to different aspects and segments of your career life.

Ask yourself: *"If based on reading this book, this theory proved true for me in at least one occasion, what makes it inapplicable in other occasions? Where was it applicable in the past, and I benefited from it? Where was it applicable, but I didn't use it?"* This is the best research you can do for yourself. Researching your life backwards will give you a new life forward, as Carl Jung stated in the following quote:

"Life really does begin at forty. Up until then, you are just doing research."

Man's biggest value is not in what happens in his life but in what he makes of what happens. So, deepening your belief that 'You Are The One And Only' is a monumental leap in transforming it from a theory to a belief to a reality. It is only then that things will conspire for you and not against you. Opportunities will uncover themselves, and occurrences will no longer seem like coincidences but rather like fate.

This faith and fate will set you free. As Roy Melvyn brilliantly puts it in his book "The Lost Writings of Wu Hsin": "The truth will not set you free. The truth will only reveal that you have always been free!"

> Man's biggest value is not in what happens in his life but in what he makes of what happens.

2) Keep Collecting

'You Are The One And Only' because of the many things you have collected over the course of your career. You are who you are now because of what you have picked up at every station, corner, and twist. The act of selecting pieces in the past, willingly or unwillingly, has turned your professional profile into the unmatched masterpiece it is today. There is no reason you should stop. In fact, there's every reason you should continue.

I could quote Steve Jobs' famous lines in almost every part of this book, but I need to stress them here from a different angle: "You can't connect the dots looking forward; you can only connect them looking backward.

So you have to trust that the dots will somehow connect in your future."

The second part of the quote is what I'm stressing here. After you're done with the 'Believe' part, your belief should (and will) only encourage you to collect more dots.

A descending snowball only gets bigger and stronger by continuously moving and collecting whatever comes its way. It's so confident that it doesn't hesitate to pick up whatever is in its path. It doesn't know how the collected combination of specs, pieces, or dots will eventually look or affect the snowball's shape, form, or structure; but it is sure they will 'somehow connect' and that the outcome will definitely be a bigger and stronger snowball.

So, keep moving, keep learning, and keep collecting pieces and "dots." You never know when you'll need them or in what way they will connect.

3) Make The Call

'You Are The One And Only', even if you haven't received 'the call'.

In Chapter 6, I talked about 'the call' that put me face to face with this very reality. The call confirmed that I was the only option for the company seeking a consultant with a unique blend of skills and expertise.

I DID own these skills and experiences BEFORE the company contacted me, and despite their call. 'The call' wasn't the reason this blend existed; it was 'the wake-up call' that it had existed long before the call was made.

The fact that you haven't received 'the call' or that no significant opportunity has presented itself to you yet, doesn't mean you are not 'The One And Only'. We have already established this in this chapter and others.

(Side note: I doubt that this hasn't happened. By revisiting and 'researching' your life, I can guarantee that you have encountered several 'calls' —not just one call— that you picked, missed, or even rejected. Yet, before reading this book, you wouldn't have called them 'One And Only' opportunities, would you?)

I want to offer you TWO reassuring reliefs. First, even if you haven't received 'the call', you're still 'The One And Only' by definition. You possess a treasure of unique and unparalleled skills and competencies. Just because the world hasn't discovered your worth yet, doesn't mean you don't own that worth or that the world doesn't need you. Your worth exists, as does the world's need for it, regardless of whether the two come together through 'the call'. This should be your basic, normal state of mind and unshakable belief.

> Just because the world hasn't discovered your worth yet, doesn't mean you don't own that worth or that the world doesn't need you.

Second, if you hold both together: 'belief' and 'keep collecting', your chances of receiving 'the call' will increase and opportunities will appear. I also have good news for you, and I want you to take it as a challenge: don't wait for the call—*make the call.*

Seize opportunities. Seek opportunities. And if there are no opportunities, create them.

Make the call.

> Seize opportunities. Seek opportunities. And if there are no opportunities, create them.

4) Unleash Your New Niche

'You Are The One And Only'. You are not the best, nor better or 'worse' than others. You are just you. And there's no you other than you. Your best bargain, therefore, is to build on who you ALREADY are and constantly strive to be better than you—and you only. (Notice I said 'build on', which means to invest in and capitalize on who you are, as opposed to being satisfied with the idea of your uniqueness but doing nothing about it.)

> 'You Are The One And Only'. You are not the best, nor better or 'worse' than others.

> You are just you. And there's no you other than you.

The alternative, which is unfortunately the common practice, is to expend our energy and life on beating and surpassing others' records and achievements to 'rank' higher and gain recognition in the media or market. That's a different game—a game that diverts your talents and abilities in the wrong direction.

You may win, and you probably will. But it's the kind of winning that requires you to continuously protect your win from being lost to another rival who seeks to surpass you, just as you did to others. That is called 'the rat race', my friend. Instead, play a different game—a game that intelligent commerce, business, and the economy engage in.

During my car's periodic service at the agency, I stopped by the desk of an auto sales representative and asked if they had any used cars for sale. I was looking for a car that my two sons could use to drive to college. The salesperson asked me a few questions, particularly about their exact needs, and he immediately suggested a small, affordable, yet reliable car that these two young men could use without putting a heavy strain on their parents' budget. I thanked him for his sincere advice and promised I would get back to him. My friend was with me as we had this conversation (he had actually come to pick me up since my car would stay at the agency for another day for service).

The moment I hopped into my friend's car, I asked him what he thought of the car suggestions. "What do you think of the deal? Is it good or bad? Is a new car better than a used car? What about so-and-so brands? I heard they are cheaper and yet equally good."

My friend—who is very close to my family and knows my children, their needs, and their father's situation—responded, "Mohamed, there is no better or worse. It depends on the particular factors and circumstances you and your sons are experiencing at the moment." He went on to analyze every angle and aspect of the situation, and we ended up convinced of a specific car option for my sons.

The interesting part was that we both agreed there are no better or worse car options. Each option is favorable for clients who see them as such. The detailed needs, limitations, abilities, and goals of each client determine the best option for that particular client. It goes without saying that every brand, every product, every model, every business solution, and every professional is a uniquely preferred solution for a particular problem or need.

Put simply and plainly: each is a niche, a unique niche. This is, no doubt, the reason the car industry (in fact, every industry) doesn't decline or dissolve despite the flooding market. If there were one-size-fits-all cars, we wouldn't have all these emerging car brands with innovative manufacturing that caters to new and developing economic, technical, and social demands.

Niche comes from French and derives from the Middle French verb *nicher*, meaning "to make a nest." *Niche* was first used in English to refer to a nook in a wall where you could display a statue or something else—like a little nest for decorative objects (Source: Dictionary.com).

Based on this, if you pay attention to evolving markets, jobs, or products, you will always be the solution to fill a gap that remains unfulfilled by a specific category of consumers and customers. As your 'keep collecting' attitude and actions expand, you'll find you synchronize easier and quicker with the constantly changing demands of the business world.

There's a famous Arabic proverb that says, "If it weren't for the diverse tastes of people, all commodities would disappear." The primary reason why trade and commerce remain the most vital backbone of society is the variety of needs, necessities, and 'nests' ready to welcome new talents and innovations.

So, there's no point in running and racing toward higher ranks or becoming better or the best. The real game of winning is when you activate your 'OAO' power to help those who need it the most. Statistically, you have infinite possibilities to succeed this way. Your collection of experiences—your 'mass of mess'—contains many valuable ingredients, allowing you to create countless unique solutions for different needs.

> Your collection of experiences—your 'mass of mess'—contains many valuable ingredients, allowing you to create countless unique solutions for different needs.

Abandon the rat race and engage in your one-of-a-kind game.

Unleash your new niche.

> Abandon the rat race and engage in your one-of-a-kind game.
> Unleash your new niche.

5) Think "Global Peace"

'You Are The One And Only'. This is the logical and natural outcome of following through the previous four points. The fifth and final point unfolds naturally. Let's do a quick recap:

- **Believe**: You believe that 'You Are The One And Only', that you always have been and always will be.
- **Keep Collecting**: You never stop learning, growing, and gathering more pieces of experience, skills, and knowledge—the very things that made you believe 'You Are The One And Only'.
- **Make The Call**: You seize, seek, and create opportunities by 'making the call' and acting on (not just settling for) the reality that 'You Are The One And Only'.
- **Unleash Your Niche:** You become more aware of what the world needs and more confident in what you can contribute. In the process, you realize that you're not just pursuing random opportunities but uncovering a unique niche for each need you see yourself fulfilling. Your belief that 'You Are The One And Only' then evolves from occasional occurrences to opportunities discovered and made deliberately.

Once you reach this stage, you have set yourself free from all the detrimental effects of the world of career, business, and vocation—the world we agreed would take up the major part of your life. By believing and living 'You Are The One And Only' day in and day out, you are now liberated from the toxic impacts of a roller coaster career life.

You are immune to the venoms that merciless rivalry exposes you to. This didn't happen by escaping or evading the world of work, but by understanding it—and before that, by understanding yourself, your worth, and your unrivaled professional profile.

You have made peace with the world of work. You are no longer scared of it, lost in it, or continually worried about your place in it. The peace you've created with your world is now ready to expand into the bigger world.

You are much wiser and more enlightened about how the universe works in perfect harmony. You can see how the intricate textures and fabrics of creation are brilliantly interwoven to coexist and function together—like the different pieces of a puzzle coming together to form one big, beautiful picture.

And you're not separate from all of that. You've solved and completed your puzzle. You've gathered all the 'pieces' of your life—the seemingly unrelated events, experiences, and encounters. You figured out how they form an unparalleled and unmatched human being, whose existence in this time and place is neither coincidental nor meaningless. You've seen how you have become part of healing many individuals and groups, and helping them overcome their complex issues thanks to the unique combination of gifts and abilities you possess.

Your solved puzzle became the missing piece in the unsolved puzzle of the bigger world.

> Your solved puzzle became the missing piece in the unsolved puzzle of the bigger world.

'You Are The One And Only', in the world of career and business—the world that, by default, is supposed to be the place where problems are solved, issues are resolved, and pain is stopped.

'You Are The One And Only' means you have replaced fear with love, struggle with serenity, and anxiety with joy in an environment that has programmed us to believe that these poisons are inevitable and must-haves. And yet, you have proved otherwise.

Yes, it's true that—like everyone else—you are a professional who goes through all sorts of challenges, ups, and downs in and because of work. But unlike everyone else, you're doing it with love, joy, and peace instead of envy, stress, and fear.

Look at you. Someone with these qualities in the world of work and business is not only a successful and peaceful professional but also an ambassador for peace!

The world of work will not only benefit from your uniqueness but will also start to learn from you and live like you. Clients will sense the sincerity and quality of the work you bring, mixed with passion and devotion. Colleagues at work will learn to be as confident and caring as you are when they witness your openness and willingness to unconditionally serve and support everyone—without the fear that your talents and gifts will be 'stolen'.

You are not afraid of anyone. You are a friend to everyone. With your inner peace of mind and outer peaceful manner with others, you create a new world that is open to more peace—a world where humans live in harmony, knowing that no one is better than others and that everyone needs everyone.

This reciprocation of services and skills is the essence of global peace. I once heard a beautiful saying by an American economist: *"Trading is the biggest peacekeeping force on Earth."* Think about that for a moment.

When 'You Are The One And Only', you are actually trading—trading your gifts for the betterment of people and societies, trading your services for a successful profession, and trading fear for love, anxiety for excitement, and struggle for serenity.

***

Ali - my - father and his friend Sagar were the perfect example of this peace. As professionals who worked together, they painted a magnificent picture of brotherhood that transcended race, religion, caste, and creed.

Bahrain embraced Sagar through Ali, and India embraced Ali through Sagar. In both cases, these two individuals taught the world how harmony among humans—all humans—can start from the very place known for its noise, turbulence, and disturbance: the workplace.

Across the borders of Bahrain, Saudi Arabia, and India, all borders have dissolved. The barriers that separate us, make us fearful of one another, and prevent us from being kind and good to each other have vanished in a moment of revelation in 2013.

Saudi Arabia awakened me to the truth I needed to know, live, and—through this book—teach to as many people as I can.

Bahrain has planted the tree of life and love that those two men have nurtured in the heart of their work.

And India has healed my father's disease, as well as a disease that threatens to spread further: distrust and destruction among the greater family of humanity.

I am The One And Only.

You are The One And Only.

Everyone is The One And Only.

When we all wake up and live up to this truth, the world will be a beautiful place, where everyone has a place.

But it has to start with us: You and I.

> When we all wake up and live up to this truth, the world will be a beautiful place, where everyone has a place.
> But it has to start with us: You and I.

A NOTE TO THE READERS

*H*i Readers,

Thank you for encouraging the writer in me, by purchasing and reading this book.

This is my first ever book and it means a lot to me that you have taken considerable time out of your busy schedule to read this book.

I would love to hear from you as to what you thought about this book, and in what way has its content motivated and moved you to take a meaningful action with your career life.

You may also be interested in my signature 5-Steps coaching program 'The One And Only'.

Please send an email to oneandonly@mohamedshukri.com.

You could also check out my profile on the Accredited Speakers listing on the Toastmasters International Page.

https://www.toastmasters.org/membership/accredited%20speaker/Accredited%20Speaker%20Profiles/Mohamed%20Ali%20Shukri

If you would like a sneak peak into my upcoming books or programs, you can stay connected through:

info@mohamedshukri.com

www.mohamedshukri.com

www.linkedin.com/in/mohamed-ali-shukri/

Thank you,

Mohamed Ali Shukri

APPENDIX

- **Accredited Speaker:** An Accredited Speaker (AS) is a prestigious designation awarded by Toastmasters International to members who demonstrate outstanding public speaking skills and proficiency. Worldwide, only around 100 accredited speakers are there as certified by Toastmasters International.

  In this link pertaining to accredited speakers, you can find the profile of Mohamed Ali Shukri.

  https://www.toastmasters.org/membership/accredited%20speaker/Accredited%20Speaker%20Profiles/Mohamed%20Ali%20Shukri

  If you wish to find an accredited speaker, here's the link

  https://www.toastmasters.org/membership/accredited-speaker/accredited%20speaker%20profiles

- **OAO: The One and Only. It is a program conceptualized by Mohamed Ali Shukri.**
- **Blue Ocean Strategy:** 'Blue Ocean Strategy' is a business framework developed by W. Chan Kim and Renée Mauborgne. The concept focuses on creating new market spaces ('blue oceans') instead of competing

in existing industries ('red oceans'), where competition is fierce and profits are low.

The cornerstone of the Blue Ocean Strategy is value innovation, which involves simultaneously pursuing differentiation and low cost, creating a leap in value for both the company and its customers.

To know more, please check this link
https://www.blueoceanstrategy.com/what-is-blue-ocean-strategy/

- **Toastmasters International**: Toastmasters International is a non-profit organization founded in 1924 by Ralph Smedley and it has its headquarters in the USA. It has a presence in 150 countries. Its aim is to help enhance the communication and leadership skills of its members. Toastmasters International has done research on communication and leadership skills enhancement and it is amongst the world's leading experiential educational services providers. 70% of the Fortune 500 organizations also recommend Toastmasters to their employees. Several Multinational Corporations have set up Toastmasters Clubs to help their employees enhance their skills. At toastmasters, members learn by doing. The members are assigned mentors to help them grow. Toastmasters operates on peer review or peer evaluation. Toastmasters provides a positive and supportive environment where members can grow and flourish as no one criticises them or makes fun of them. Rather, the members are provided with evaluations which are intended to motivate. For further details, please refer,

https://www.toastmasters.org

Photos of my father in India

Dad with my brother, in our early days arriving in Mumbai (April 2013).

Dr. Omar updates me on dad's condition in his clinic in Mumbai.

Dad finally meets his old colleague and buddy Sagar in Mangalore.

Dad with Dr. Sahil Bantwal before the operation in Unity Hospital, Mangalore.

Dad being discharged from Unity Hospital, Mangalore, fully recovered.

In a textile shop in Colaba, Mumbai. Dad's unsurprising habit to instantly engage with different people, whoever they are and wherever they come from, taught me to see the world as a beautiful fabric woven by love and friendship.

Dad in 'Mani Bhavan' (Jewel house) in Mumbai: a museum and historical building dedicated to Mahatma Gandhi (the leader of the Indian Independence Movement against British rule, and as such considered as the father of the nation). In the image, dad is standing where Gandhi's statue is holding and leaning on a stick. It is as if the 'father of India' is saying to my father: "I am relying on you, Ali, to spread love and peace" – which is something dad led by example. And, in this photo, my father is looking at me, and whoever reads this book, saying:

"Son, spread the word of peace and love. BE THE CHANGE YOU WANT TO SEE IN THE WORLD."

You Are The One And Only

www.ingramcontent.com/pod-product-compliance
Lightning Source LLC
LaVergne TN
LVHW041942070526
838199LV00051BA/2881